FIRSTHAND HISTORY

Publisher's Note

Firsthand History: Jamestown to Washington's Farewell 1607-1801 *gathers the first three booklets of a series that was published by McGraw Hill in the 1960s entitled* Voices from America's Past. *Careful effort has been made to adhere to the original text. The diaries, letters, biographies, and narratives that the editors collected illumine not only the circumstances, but the beliefs and assumptions of their authors. In the same way, the editors' commentary, some sixty years since it was first published, is itself an historical document that reveals a great deal about the framework that academics of that era imposed on their reading of history. Indeed, what the editors chose to include is as telling as what they omitted from this compilation.*

If some of the terms or observations in the commentary give contemporary readers pause it is a measure of the sea change that has been taking place since it was written. While by no means comprehensive, the following material offers fascinating stuff with which to supplement an understanding of United States history.

FIRSTHAND HISTORY
Jamestown to Washington's Farewell 1607-1801

EDITED BY
RICHARD B. MORRIS AND JAMES WOODRESS

Warbler Press

First published by Webster Division, McGraw-Hill Book Company a part of a series entitled *Voices from America's Past*, 1961

This edition gathers the complete text of *The Beginnings of America 1607-1763*, *The Times That Tried Men's Souls 1770-1783*, and *The Age of Washington 1783-1801*

Excerpt from *Of Plymouth Plantation*, by William Bradford, edited by Samuel Eliot Morison reprinted by permission of Alfred Knopf, Inc., 1952. Poems by Edward Taylor, "Housewifery" and "The Joy of Church Fellowship Rightly Attended" reprinted by permission of the *New England Quarterly*, December, 1937. Account by the Reverend Jonas Clark, from Charles Hudson's *History of the Town of Lexington, Massachusetts* was reprinted by permission of the Lexington Historical Society. Letter by Samuel Adams, from the *Warren-Adams Letters* reprinted by permission of the Massachusetts Historical Society. Account by Ambrose Serle from *The American Journal of Ambrose Serle* reprinted by permission of the Huntington Library, San Marino, California.

All rights reserved. No part of this book may be reproduced in any form or by any means, electronic or mechanical, including photocopying, recording, or by any information storage and retrieval system, without permission from the publisher, which may be requested at permissions@warblerpress.com.

ISBN 978-1-7348526-5-3 (paperback)
ISBN 978-1-7348526-6-0 (e-book)

warblerpress.com

Printed in the United States of America. This edition is printed with chlorine-free ink on acid-free interior paper made from 30% post-consumer waste recycled material.

Contents

Publisher's Note 11

PART ONE
THE BEGINNINGS OF AMERICA 1607-1763
Preface 3
I. Settlements North and South 5
    The Founding of Jamestown 5
    The Founding of Plymouth 14
II. Religious Life in America 29
    New England 29
    Other Colonies 42
III. Colonial Problems 46
    Indian Troubles 46
    Conflict with France 52
IV. Colonial Life 56
    Transportation 56
    Life in the South 59
    Life in a City 64

PART TWO
THE TIMES THAT TRIED MEN'S SOULS 1770-1783
Preface 73
I. The Foreground 76
    The Boston Massacre 76
    The Boston Tea Party 79

| Paul Revere's Ride 85
| The Battle of Lexington 90
| The Battle of Concord 94
| The Capture of Ticonderoga 96
| II. Behind the Lines 101
| Defiant Words 101
| The Problem of the Loyalist 108
| III. The Major Battles and Trials 113
| The Battle of Long Island 113
| Washington's Retreat 116
| Burgoyne's Surrender at Saratoga 119
| Valley Forge 123
| John Paul Jones Defeats the *Serapis* 125
| Benedict Arnold's Treason 127
| The End of the War: Yorktown 131
| IV. Winning the Peace 135
| Negotiations and Reflections 135

PART THREE
THE AGE OF WASHINGTON 1783-1801
Preface 143
I. Life in America After the Revolution 145
    Emigration Reports 145
    Yellow Fever Strikes Philadelphia 152
II. The Days of Confederation 156
    The Articles 156
    Shays' Rebellion 159
    Westward Expansion 163
    Foreign Affairs 169
III. The Constitution 173
    The Convention at Work 173
    Signing the Constitution 180
    Ratifying the Constitution 183
IV. Washington's Administration 186

    Jefferson's Views of Hamilton and the Administration ... 186
    Hamilton's View of Jefferson 189
    The Jay Treaty 190
    The Barbary Pirates 192
V. The Adams Administration 198
    Washington's Farewell Address....................... 198
    The XYZ Affair 200
    The Alien and Sedition Acts 204

About the Editors.. 209

PART ONE

The Beginnings of America
1607-1763

Preface

The seventeenth century in America was the seedtime of colonization. For 115 years after Columbus discovered America, explorers sailed the western waters, and the nations of Europe staked out vast empires. England launched several successful attempts to plant colonies in what is now the United States. In the years following the landing at Jamestown in 1607, England laid the foundation for her extensive colonial system in North America. From these scattered colonies a nation grew, but a long time passed before the colonies became states and the states became a nation.

The English colonization of North America did not suffer for want of reporters to describe it. The people who took part in the enterprise wrote a great deal about their experiences. Governor Bradford of Plymouth wrote a history to preserve a record of the colony's early days. Captain John Smith of Virginia wrote pamphlets to satisfy the curiosity of folks back home who might want to come to the New World. Many of these works were printed immediately; others remained in manuscript until our day.

Not only the leaders of the colonies wrote of their deeds. Ordinary people also sent letters home to England and kept diaries for their personal satisfaction. All in all, the United States had her beginnings amid ample publicity. We are grateful to these people for preserving records of the early days, for through their efforts we can get a first-hand idea of colonial times. We don't have to guess about the events that took place in America three hundred years ago. Of course, we don't have nearly as many documents as we could wish for, but we do have plenty of records to draw upon.

This is the first of a series of booklets containing the story of America, as told by those who were there, the eyewitnesses and participants. The selections which make up this booklet are a few of the records that historians use in writing their books. These diaries, letters, biographies, and narratives are the raw material of history. These accounts bring us face to face with the Indians of Virginia in 1607, make us feel something of the sufferings of the Pilgrims in Massachusetts during their "starving time," tell us about the deep religious beliefs of the colonists, and the superstitions, like witchcraft, which were hard to root out. We see life through the eyes of a prosperous planter in Virginia and a struggling printer's apprentice in Philadelphia. History books can provide over-all pictures of a country's development, but these eyewitness accounts and first-hand reports put flesh on the bare bones of history.

In editing this booklet, we have let the authors tell their own story in their own words, but we have sometimes modernized the spelling and punctuation and-when it seemed absolutely necessary-words and sentence structure. Our aim has been to turn the language of these old documents into English modern enough that what the writers have to say is not obscured by the way they said it. Occasionally we have made cuts within selections to save space, but, for the most part, the material used is complete.

Richard B. Morris
James Woodress

I. Settlements North and South

THE FOUNDING OF JAMESTOWN

The first permanent English settlement in America was founded at Jamestown, Virginia, in May, 1607. The colonists who went ashore that spring morning more than three and one-half centuries ago discovered no cultivated countryside. Instead of the trim, green farms one sees along the James River today, they found a howling wilderness full of hostile Indians and wild beasts. Neither the colonists nor their merchant-sponsors in England were prepared for the troubles that Jamestown faced. The settlers died of disease, starvation, and Indian attacks, and they quarreled endlessly among themselves. The stockholders in the Virginia Company never made any money on their investment in the colony.

The Jamestown settlers sailed from England in three ships on December 19, 1606. Captain Christopher Newport was in charge of getting the colonists to Virginia. The ships stopped in the Canary Islands and the West Indies before reaching their destination. It was a long, exhausting voyage. Several weeks after landing at Jamestown, Captain Newport returned to England. The settlers then were on their own.

The following account of the early days at Jamestown was compiled in London by William Simmonds. It is based on the writings, freely adapted, of several of the colonists who were his friends. As you can see, Simmonds' friends had no use for Edward

Wingfield, the first president of the colony. They were supporters of Captain John Smith, whose own writings begin after this narrative.

BEING thus left to our fortunes, within ten days, scarce ten amongst us could either go or well stand, such extreme weakness and sickness oppressed us. And thereat none need marvel, if they consider the cause and reason, which was this: whilst the ships stayed, our allowance of food was somewhat bettered by a daily portion of biscuit which the sailors would pilfer [steal] to sell, give, or exchange with us, for money, sassafras, [or] furs....But when they departed, there remained neither tavern, beer house, nor place of relief but the common kettle.

Had we been as free from all sins as we were free from gluttony and drunkenness, we might have been canonized for saints. But our president would never have been admitted, for he kept for his private use oatmeal, sack [wine], oil, aqua vitae [brandy], beef, eggs, or what not. [President Wingfield hotly denied this charge.] The [contents of the common] kettle indeed he allowed equally to be distributed, and that was half a pint of wheat and as much barley boiled with water for a man a day. This [grain] having fried some 26 weeks in the ship's hold contained as many worms as grains, so that we might truly call it rather so much bran than corn.

Our drink was water, our lodging, castles in the air. With this lodging and diet our extreme toil in bearing and planting palisades strained and bruised us. Our continual labor in the extremity of the heat had so weakened us as were cause sufficient to have made us miserable in our native country, or any other place in the world. From May to September those that escaped dying lived upon sturgeon and sea crabs. Fifty in this time we buried. [The original colony numbered 104.]

Then seeing the President's projects (who all this time had neither felt want nor sickness) to escape these miseries by flight in our pinnace [small sailing boat] so moved our dead spirits that we deposed [removed] him and established [John] Ratcliffe in his place....But now was all our provision spent, the sturgeon gone, all helps abandoned, each hour expecting the fury of the savages, when God, the patron of all good endeavors, in that desperate extremity, so changed the hearts of the savages that they brought such plenty of their fruits and provision that no man wanted.

And now where some affirmed it was ill done of the Council to send forth men so badly provided, this incontradictable reason will show them plainly they are too ill-advised to nourish such ideas. First, the fault of our going was our own. What could be thought fitting or necessary we had; but what we should find, what we should want, where we should be, we were all ignorant. And supposing to make our passage in two months with victual [food] to live and the advantage of spring to work, we were at sea five months where we spent both our victual and lost the opportunity of the time and season to plant.

Such actions have ever since the world's beginning been subject to such accidents. Everything of worth is found full of difficulties, but nothing [is] so difficult as to establish a commonwealth so far remote from men and means and where men's minds are so untoward [unlucky] as neither [to] do well themselves nor to suffer others [to do well]. But to proceed.

The new president, being little beloved, of weak judgment in dangers and less industry in peace, committed the managing of all things abroad to Captain Smith, who, by his own example, good words, and fair promises set some to mow, others to bind thatch, some to build houses, others to thatch them, himself always bearing the greatest task for his own share. In short time he provided most of them lodgings, neglecting any for himself.

This done, seeing the savages' superfluity [large numbers] begin to decrease, [he] with some of his workmen shipped himself in the shallop [small boat] to search the country for trade....He went down the river to Kecoughtan [an Indian village] where at first they scorned him as a starved man, yet he so dealt with them that the next day they loaded his boat with corn. And in his return he discovered and kindly traded with the Warascoyks....

And now the winter approaching, the rivers became so covered with swans, geese, ducks, and cranes that we daily feasted with good bread, Virginia peas, pumpkins, and persimmons, fish, fowl, and diverse sorts of wild beasts...so that none of our Tuftaffaty [silk-dressed] humorists desired to go for England.

John Smith 1580-1631

Captain John Smith already had lived an exciting life by the time he joined the Virginia-bound colonists at the age of 26. He had left England at 16 to become a soldier of fortune on the continent of Europe. He fought with the Austrians against the Turks, and once in single combat he cut off the heads of three Turkish champions. A Transylvanian prince rewarded him with a coat of arms for his deeds. Later he was captured and given as a present to the wife of a Turkish pasha, but he escaped and made his way back to England.

Smith's adventures are so fantastic that many historians have called him a liar and refused to believe him. Yet recent historical research shows that Smith's stories are reasonably accurate. He may have exaggerated his adventures to make a good story a little better, but it is probably true that Smith saved the Jamestown colony by his resourceful foraging among the Indians and by his bold leadership. Certainly he was an energetic and able man. For a fascinating account of Smith's career, as verified by an expert in Hungarian history, see Marshall Fishwick, "Was John Smith a Liar?" *American Heritage*, IX, 29-33, 110 (October, 1958).

Smith returned to England in 1609 and never again saw Virginia, but he wrote much about the colony. One of his most interesting works is a pamphlet called A Mop of Virginia. In it he put together a vivid eyewitness account of the animals, the plants, and the Indians. Smith's booklet was designed to satisfy the great curiosity in England about the New World and to urge new settlers to go there. He does not mention the hardships.

THE INDIANS

THE people differ very much in stature...some being very great... others very little...but generally tall and straight, of a comely [pretty] proportion and of a color brown, when they are of any age, but they are borne white. Their hair is generally black, but few have any beards. The men wear half their heads shaven, the other half long. For barbers they use their women, who with two shells will grate the hair, of any fashion they please....

They are very strong, of an able body and full of agility, able to endure, to lie in the woods under a tree by the fire in the worst of winter or in the weeds and grass in ambush in the summer. They are inconstant [changeable] in everything but what fear constrains them to keep....Some are of disposition fearful, some bold, most cautelous [deceitful], all savage. Generally [they are] covetous of copper, beads, and such like trash. They are soon moved to anger and so malicious that they seldom forget an injury....

For their apparel they are sometimes covered with skins of wild beasts, which in winter are dressed with the hair but in summer without. The better sort use large mantles of deerskin...some embroidered with white beads, some with copper, others painted after their manner. But the common sort have scarce to cover their nakedness but with grass, the leaves of trees, or such like. We have seen some use mantles made of turkey feathers so prettily wrought and woven with threads that nothing could be discerned [seen] but the feathers, that was exceedingly warm and very handsome. But the women are always covered about their middles with a skin and very shamefast to be seen bare....

Their women some have their legs, hands, breasts, and face cunningly embroidered with diverse works, as beasts, serpents, artificially wrought into their flesh with black spots. In each ear commonly they have three great holes, whereat they hang chains, bracelets, or copper. Some of their men wear in those holes a small green and yellow colored snake, near half a yard in length, which crawling and lapping herself about his neck often times familiarly would kiss his lips. Others wear a dead rat tied by the tail. Some on their heads wear the wing of a bird or some large feather with a rattle....Their heads and shoulders are painted red with the root pocone powdered and mixed with oil; this they hold in summer to preserve them from the heat and in winter from the cold. Many other forms of paintings they use, but he is the most gallant that is the most monstrous to behold....

Men, women, and children have their several names according to the several humors of their parents. Their women (they say) are easily delivered of child, yet do they love children very dearly. To make them hardy, in the coldest mornings they wash them in the rivers and by painting and ointments so tan their skins that after a year or two no weather will hurt them.

The men bestow their time in fishing, hunting, wars, and such man-like exercises...which is the cause that the women be very painful [busy] and the men often idle. The women and children do the rest of the work. They make mats, baskets, pots, pound their corn, make their bread, prepare their victuals, plant their corn, gather their corn, bear all kinds of burdens, and such like.

Their fire they kindle presently by chafing a dry pointed stick in a hole of a little square piece of wood, that firing itself will so fire moss, leaves, or any such like dry thing that will quickly burn.

THEIR RELIGION

THERE is yet in Virginia no place discovered to be so savage in which the savages have not a religion, deer, and bow and arrows. All things that were able to do them hurt beyond their prevention they adore with their kind of divine worship, as the fire, water, lightning, thunder, our ordnance [guns], horses, etc. But their chief god they worship is the devil. Him they call Oke and serve him more of fear than love. They say they have conference with him and fashion themselves as near to his shape as they can imagine. In their temples, they have his image evil favoredly carved and then painted and adorned with chains, copper, and beads, and covered with a skin....

By him is commonly the sepulchre [tomb] of their kings. Their bodies are first bowelled [that is, disembowelled or the internal organs removed], then dried upon hurdles [racks] till they be very dry, and so about the most of their joints and neck they hang bracelets or chains of copper, pearl, and such like, as they used to wear. Their inwards they stuff with copper beads and cover with a skin, hatchets, and such trash. Then they lappe [wrap] them very carefully in white skins and so roll them in mats for their winding sheets. And in the tomb, which is an arch made of mats, they lay them orderly. What remaineth of this kind of wealth their kings have, they set at their feet in baskets. These temples and bodies are kept by their priests.

For their ordinary burials they dig a deep hole in the earth with sharp stakes, and the corpses being lapped in skins and mats with their jewels, they lay them upon sticks in the ground and so cover them with earth. The burial ended, the women being painted all their faces with black coal and oil do sit 24 hours in the houses mourning and lamenting by turns with such yelling and howling as may express their great passions.

John Smith's most famous story is the account of his rescue by Pocahontas, but many historians have doubted the tale. Smith is the only person who says it happened. The facts are these: During the first hard winter, 1607-1608, when Smith was scouting for provisions, he was captured by the Indians and taken to the chief,

Powhatan, father of Pocahontas. After three weeks the chief sent him back to Jamestown. When Smith first wrote about his experiences a few months later, he never mentioned Pocahontas.

Years later, in England, Smith wrote a history of Virginia and, for the first time, told the story of Pocahontas. Between the time Smith was captured and the time he wrote his history, Pocahontas had married an Englishman. Her husband had brought her to England, where she had been a sensation. One cannot help feeling that Smith "remembered" more than actually happened in order to exploit public interest in the Indian princess. His account, however, is a good story, even if it happened only in his mind. Pocahontas was a real person who visited Jamestown often and brought food to the starving settlers during their worst times. Many Americans like to think the episode is true, and the tale has become part of our folklore, like the legendary deeds of Davy Crockett. Here is Smith's story:

At last they brought him [note that here Smith writes of himself in the third person] to Meronocomoco where was Powhatan, their emperor. Here more than two hundred of those grim courtiers stood wondering at him, as he had been a monster....Before a fire upon a seat like a bedstead he sat covered with a great robe made of raccoon skins and all the tails hanging by. On either hand did sit a young wench of 16 or 18 years, and along on each side [of] the house two rows of men, and behind them as many women, with all their heads and shoulders painted red. Many of their heads [were] bedecked with the white down of birds; but everyone with something, and a great chain of white beads about their necks.

At his entrance before the king, all the people gave a great shout. The Queen of Appamatuck was appointed to bring him water to wash his hands, and another brought him a bunch of feathers instead of a towel to dry them. Having feasted him after their best barbarous manner they could, a long consultation was held, but the conclusion was [that] two great stones were brought before Powhatan. Then as many as could, laid hands on him, dragged him to them, and thereon laid his head, and being ready with their clubs to beat out his brains, Pocahontas, the king's dearest daughter, when no entreaty could prevail, got his head in her arms and laid her own upon his to save him from death; whereat the emperor was contented he should live to make him hatchets, and her bells, beads, and copper; for they thought him as well [capable] of all occupations as themselves. For the king himself will make his own robes, shoes, bows, arrows, pots; plant, hunt, or do anything so well as the rest....

Two days after, Powhatan having disguised himself in the most fearfullest manner he could, caused Captain Smith to be brought forth to a great house in the woods, and there upon u mat by the fire to be left alone. Not long after from behind a mat that divided the house was made the most dolefullest noise he ever heard. Then Powhatan, more like a devil than a man, with some two hundred more as black as himself, came unto him and told him now they were friends and presently he should go to Jamestown....So to Jamestown with 12 guides Powhatan sent him.

In another place in the history, Smith prints a letter he wrote to the Queen of England at the time Pocahontas visited London. In this letter he tells more about the Indian girl and describes her as a sort of guardian angel for the colony:

[Pocahontas] so prevailed with her father that I was safely conducted to Jamestown, where I found about eight and thirty miserable poor and sick creatures to keep possession of all those large territories of Virginia; such was the weakness of this poor commonwealth. Had the savages not fed us, we directly had starved. And this relief, most gracious Queen, was commonly brought us by this Lady Pocahontas.

Notwithstanding all these passages, when inconstant fortune

turned our peace to war, this tender virgin would still not spare to dare to visit us, and by her our jars [distresses] have been oft appeased and our wants still supplied. Were it the policy of her father thus to employ her or the ordinance of God thus to make her His instrument, or her extraordinary affection to our nation, I know not, but of this I am sure; when her father with the utmost of his policy and power sought to surprise me, having but 18 with me, the dark night could not affright her from coming through the irksome wood; and with watered eyes [she] gave me intelligence with her best advice to escape his fury, which had he known he had surely slain her.

Jamestown with her wild train she as freely frequented as her father's habitation, and during the time of two or three years she next under God was still the instrument to preserve this colony from death, famine, and utter confusion.

THE FOUNDING OF PLYMOUTH

William Bradford (1590-1657) was the wise and able governor of the Plymouth colony for thirty years. During this time he wrote the best account we have of our colonial beginnings. His narrative, Of Plymouth Plantation, as he called his work, is a great adventure story. The account of the little band of Pilgrims who come to Massachusetts in 1620 is filled with hardships, suffering, courage, and faith. The Pilgrims faced problems hard to solve, for they landed on the bleak coast of New England at the beginning of the winter. They were three thousand miles from home, friends, and civilization, but they worked, prayed, and survived. The leadership of William Bradford is one of the reasons that the Plymouth settlers were able to survive on the rocky shores of Massachusetts.

Governor Bradford began his history of the colony soon after the landing and worked on it, from time to time, for many years. The precious manuscript was not published, but was kept in the family. Early historians used it, and at the time of the Revolution it was kept in the library of the Old South Church in Boston. During the war the manuscript was stolen, probably by a British soldier, and was lost for years. In the middle of the nineteenth century, however, it was found in the library of the Bishop of London. Various Americans tried to persuade the British to return the historic document to America. Finally the American ambassador succeeded in bringing the manuscript home in 1897, and it now is the property of the Commonwealth of Massachusetts.

If the manuscript were printed just as it was written, it would look very strange. Bradford did not prepare it for publication, and thus used many abbreviations and strange contractions. Also, the English language has changed since the history was written. The following selections have been pruned somewhat and words have been spelled out, but the governor's old-fashioned language is still not easy to read. Be patient and you will understand it. It is a story of simple faith and courage.

The first part of the history describes the experiences of the Pilgrims before they came to America. Because they disapproved of the Church of England, they separated themselves from it. Hence the Pilgrims also are known as Separatists. They first went to Holland, where they were able to worship as they pleased. But that country was small and overpopulated. They found it difficult to make a living there. Also, they feared their children would grow up more Dutch than English. Therefore they decided, after much discussion, to leave Europe for America. It was a hard decision, and some of the Pilgrims were terrified at the prospect.

Some were afraid of the long sea voyage; others were afraid they would starve to death. They worried about the change of air, diet, and drinking water. They were fearful of the Indians and intimidated by the stories they had heard. The Indians were said to be cruel, barbarous, treacherous—even cannibal. But men like Bradford argued that "all great and honorable actions were accompanied with great difficulties." It was granted that the difficulties were great and the dangers numerous. But with the aid of God and courage and patience they would overcome the obstacles. The brave ones persuaded most of the rest to go.

Thus they hired the Mayflower, a ship only ninety feet long, and left Europe on September 6, 1620. For more than nine weeks they sailed westward. At first they had fair winds, but then the autumn storms caught them and the ship began to leak. Many of the crew wanted to turn back, but emergency repairs were made, and Governor Bradford says: "They committed themselves to the will of God and resolved to proceed." Then he continues:

AFTER long beating at sea they fell with that land which is called Cape Cod; the which being made and certainly known to be it, they were not a little joyful. After some deliberation had amongst themselves and with the master of the ship, they tacked about and resolved to stand for the southward (the wind and weather being fair) to find some place about Hudson's River for their habitation. But after they had sailed that course about half the day, they fell amongst dangerous shoals and roaring breakers, and they were so far entangled therewith as they conceived themselves in great danger; and the wind shrinking upon them withal, they resolved to bear up again for the Cape, and thought themselves happy to get out of those dangers before night overtook them, as by God's good providence they did.

Being thus arrived in a good harbor, and brought safe to land, they fell upon their knees and blessed the God of Heaven, who had brought them over the vast and furious ocean, and delivered them from all the perils and miseries thereof, again to set their feet on the firm and stable earth....

But here I cannot but stay and make a pause, and stand half amazed at this poor people's present condition; and so I think will the reader, too, when he well considers the same. Being thus passed the vast ocean, and a sea of troubles before in their preparation, they had now no friends to welcome them nor inns to entertain or refresh their weatherbeaten bodies; no houses or much less towns to repair to, to seek for succour [help]. It is recorded in Scripture as a mercy to the Apostle and his shipwrecked company that the barbarians showed them no small kindness in refreshing them, but these savage barbarians, when they met with them were readier to fill their sides full of arrows than otherwise. And for the season it was winter, and they that know the winters of that country know them to be sharp and violent, and subject to cruel and fierce storms, dangerous to travel to known places, much more to search an unknown coast.

Besides, what could they see but a hideous and desolate wilderness, full of wild beasts and wild men—and what multitudes there might be of them they knew not. Neither could they, as it were, go up to the top of Pisgah [the mountain that Moses climbed to see the Promised Land] to view from this wilderness a more goodly country to feed their hopes; for which way soever they turned their eyes (save upward to the heavens) they could have little solace or content in respect of any outward objects. For summer being done, all things stand upon them with a weather-beaten face, and the whole country, full of woods and thickets, represented a wild and savage hue. If they looked behind them, there was the mighty ocean which they had passed and was now as a main bar and gulf to separate them from all the civil parts of the world....

What could now sustain them but the Spirit of God and His grace? May not and ought not the children of these fathers rightly say: "Our fathers were Englishmen which came over this great ocean, and were ready to perish in this wilderness; but they cried unto the Lord, and He heard their voice and looked on their adversity," etc. "Let them therefore praise the Lord, because He is good; and His mercies endure forever. Yea, let them which have been redeemed of the Lord, show how He hath delivered them from the hand of the oppressor. When they wandered in the desert wilderness out of the way, and found no city to dwell in, both hungry and thirsty, their soul was overwhelmed in them. Let them confess before the Lord His loving kindness and His wonderful works before the sons of men."

For the next three weeks the Pilgrims explored Cape Cod, looking for a suitable place to land and build their homes. They found Plymouth Bay and sailed the Mayflower into it on December 16. On Christmas Day, 1620, they began to erect the first house. But during their explorations they were attacked by the Indians. This was on December 6:

So they [the exploring party] ranged up and down all that day, but found no people, nor any place they liked. When the sun grew low, they hasted out of the woods to meet with their shallop [small boat], to whom they made signs to come to them into a creek hard by, which they did at high water; of which they were very glad, for they had not seen each other all that day since the morning. So they made them a barricade as usually they did every night, with logs, stakes and thick pine boughs, the height of a man, leaving it open to leeward, partly to shelter them from the cold and wind (making their fire in the middle and lying round about it) and partly to defend them from any sudden assaults of the savages, if they should surround them; so being very weary, they betook them to rest. But about midnight they heard a hideous and great cry, and their sentinel called, "Arm! arm!" So they bestirred them and stood to their arms and shot off a couple of muskets, and then the noise ceased....

So they rested till about five of the clock in the morning; for the tide, and their purpose to go from thence, made them be stirring betimes [early]. So after prayer they prepared for breakfast, and it being day dawning, it was thought best to be carrying things down to the boat. But some said it was not best to carry the arms down; others said they would be the readier, for they had lapped [wrapped] them up in their coats [as protection] from the dew; but some three or four would not carry theirs till they went themselves. Yet as it fell out, the water being not high enough, they laid them down on the bank side and came up to breakfast.

But presently, all on the sudden, they heard a great and strange cry, which they knew to be the same voices they heard in the night, though they varied their notes; and one of their company being abroad came running in and cried, "Men, Indians! Indians!" And withal, their arrows came flying amongst them. Their men ran with all speed to recover their arms, as by the good providence of God they did. In the meantime, of those that were there ready, two muskets were discharged at them, and two more stood ready in the entrance of their rendezvous but were commanded not to shoot till they could take full aim at them. And the other two charged again with all speed, for there were only four [who] had arms there, and defended the barricade, which was first assaulted.

The cry of the Indians was dreadful, especially when they saw there men run out of the rendezvous toward the shallop to recover their arms, the Indians wheeling about upon them. But some running out with coats of mail on, and cutlasses in their hands, they soon got their arms and let fly amongst them and quickly stopped their violence. Yet there was a lusty_ man, and no less valiant, [who] stood behind a tree within half a musket shot, and let his arrows fly at them; he was seen [to] shoot three arrows, which were all avoided.

He stood three shots of a musket, till one taking full aim at him made the bark or splinters of the tree fly about his ears, after which he gave an extraordinary shriek and away they went, all of them....

Thus it pleased God to vanquish their enemies and give them deliverance; and by His special providence so to dispose that not any one of them were either hurt or hit, though their arrows came close by them and on every side [of] them; and sundry [several] of their coats, which hung up in the barricade, were shot through and through. Afterwards they gave God solemn thanks and praise for their deliverance, and gathered up a bundle of their arrows and sent them into England afterward by the master of the ship, and called that place the First Encounter.

THE STARVING TIME

But that which was most sad and lamentable was, that in two or three months' time half of their company died, especially in January and February, being the depth of winter, and wanting houses and other comforts; being infected with the scurvy and other diseases which this long voyage and their inaccommodate [unfit] condition had brought upon them. So as there died sometimes two or three of a day in the foresaid time, that of 100 and odd persons, scarce fifty remained. And of these, in the time of most distress, there was but six or seven sound persons who to their great commendations, be it spoken, spared no pains night nor day, but with abundance of toil and hazard of their own health fetched them wood, made them fires, dressed them meat, made their beds, washed their loathsome clothes, clothed and unclothed them; in a word, did all the homely and necessary offices for them which dainty and queasy stomachs cannot endure to hear named; and all this willingly and cheerfully, without any grudging in the least, showing herein their true love unto their friends and brethren; a rare example and worthy to be remembered.

Two of these seven were Mr. William Brewster, their reverend Elder [Brewster conducted religious services during the early days of the Plymouth colony, though he was not an ordained minister], and Myles Standish, their Captain and military commander, unto whom myself and many others were much beholden [indebted] in our low and sick condition. And yet the Lord so upheld these persons as in this general calamity they were not at all infected either with sickness or lameness. And what I have said of these I may say of many others who died in this general visitation, and others yet living, that whilst they had health, yea, or any strength continuing, they were not wanting to any that had need of them. And I doubt not but their recompense is with the Lord.

SQUANTO

All this while the Indians came skulking about them, and would sometimes show themselves aloof off, but when any approached near them, they would run away; and once they stole away their tools where they had been at work and were gone to dinner. But about the 16th of March, a certain Indian came boldly amongst them and spoke to them in broken English, which they could well understand but marveled at it. At length they understood by discourse with him that he was not of these parts, but belonged to the eastern parts where some English ships came to fish, with whom he was acquainted and could name sundry of them by their names, amongst whom he had got his language. He became profitable to them in acquainting them with many things concerning the state of the country in the east parts where he lived....His name was Samaset. He told them also of another Indian whose name was Squanto, a native of this place, who had been in England and could speak better English than himself.

Being, after some time of entertainment and gifts dismissed, a while after he came again, and five more with him, and they brought again all the tools that were stolen away before, and made way for the coming of their great Sachem [chief], called Massasoit, who, about four or five days after, came with the chief [part] of his friends and other attendance, with the aforesaid Squanto....

Squanto continued with them and was their interpreter and was a special instrument sent of God for their good beyond their expectation. He directed them how to set [plant] their corn, where to take fish, and to procure other commodities, and was also their pilot to bring them to unknown places for their profit, and never left them till he died.

THE FIRST THANKSGIVING

THEY began now to gather in the small harvest they had, and to fit up their houses and dwellings against winter, being all well recovered in health and strength and had all things in good plenty. For as some were thus employed in affairs abroad, others were exercised in fishing, about cod and bass and other fish, of which they took good store, of which every family had their portion. All the summer there was no want; and now began to come in store of fowl, as winter approached, of which this place did abound when they came first....And besides waterfowl there was great store of wild turkeys, of which they took many, besides venison, etc. Besides they had about a peck of meal a week to a person, or now since harvest, Indian corn to that proportion. Which made many afterwards write so largely of their plenty here to their friends in England, which were not feigned [pretended] but true reports.

———•———

> Governor Bradford's history does not describe the first Thanksgiving dinner, but we have a letter written by Edward Winslow to a friend in England, in which Winslow gives details of the feast that followed the harvest. Governor Bradford sent out four hunters who returned with enough wild fowl to last the colony a week. The Pilgrims then held a celebration which was attended by Massasoit and ninety of his braves. The Indians contributed five deer for the feast, which lasted three days.
>
> Soon afterwards, however, another shipload of settlers arrived on the Fortune. The new colonists came without equipment and provisions. In order to feed the newcomers the Plymouth colony had to go on half rations for the following winter. Next, the colony had more Indian trouble, not with (Massasoit's friendly tribe, but with the Narragansett Indians. In the following selection from Bradford's history the Governor summarizes the end of 1621, the first full year of the colony:

SOON after this ship's [the *Fortune's*] departure, the great people of the Narragansetts, in a braving manner, sent a messenger unto them with a bundle of arrows tied about with a great snakeskin, which their interpreters told them was a threatening and a challenge. Upon which the Governor, with the advice of others, sent them a round answer that if they had rather have war than peace, they might begin when they would; they had done them no wrong, neither did they fear them or should they find them unprovided [unprepared]. And by another messenger [he] sent the snakeskin back with bullets in it. But they would not receive it, but sent it back again....

But this made them [the settlers] the more carefully to look to themselves, so as they agreed to enclose their dwellings with a good strong pale [fence], and make flankers [fortifications] in convenient places with gates to shut, which were every night locked, and a watch kept; and when need required, there was also warding [guarding] in the daytime. And the company was by the Captain's and the Governor's advice divided into four squadrons, and everyone had their quarter appointed them, unto which they were to repair upon any sudden alarm. And if there should be any cry of fire, a company were appointed for a guard, with muskets, whilst others quenched the same, to prevent Indian treachery. This was accomplished very cheerfully, and the town impaled round by the beginning of March [1622], in which every family had a pretty garden plot secured.

John Winthrop 1588-1649

The Puritans who settled Boston in 1630 came to the New World with plenty of supplies and equipment. There were more than a thousand new colonists in the Massachusetts Bay settlements by the end of the year. These people had the strength of numbers and did not suffer the terrible privations of the Plymouth colony, but they still had to beat back the wilderness and squeeze a living from the thin soil of New England.

What William Bradford was to the Plymouth colony, John Winthrop was to Massachusetts Bay. Both colonies were fortunate in having good, resourceful governors. John Winthrop was re-elected governor many times between the time his flagship, the *Arbella*, dropped anchor in Boston harbor and his death in 1649.

The two selections which follow pertain to Governor Winthrop. The first is part of Cotton Mather's biographical sketch of the governor. It comes from Mather's Magnolia Christi Americana (1702), which means the "American Annals of Christ." Cotton Mather himself was a famous Puritan minister, the grandson of one of the early settlers and a historian of the colony. The other selection consists of two of John Winthrop's letters to his wife, who remained in England until after the colony was established.

These are touching letters that show the wise governor as a loving husband and a devout Christian.

MATHER'S SKETCH OF WINTHROP

ACCORDINGLY when the noble design of carrying a colony of chosen people into an American wilderness was by some eminent persons undertaken, this eminent person was, by the consent of all, chosen for the Moses who must be the leader of so great an undertaking. And indeed nothing but a Mosaic spirit could have carried him through the temptations to which either his farewell to his own land or his travel in a strange land must needs expose a gentleman of his education. Wherefore having sold a fair estate of six or seven hundred [pounds] a year, he transported himself with the effects of it into New England in the year 1630, where he spent it upon the service of a famous plantation founded and formed for the seat of the most reformed Christianity....

But at the same time his liberality unto the needy was even beyond measure generous....'Twas his custom also to send some of his family upon errands unto the houses of the poor about their meal time on purpose to spy whether they wanted; and if it were found that they wanted, he would make that the opportunity of sending supplies unto them. And there was one passage of his charity that was perhaps a little unusual. In an hard and long winter, when wood was very scarce at Boston, a man gave him a private information that a needy person in the neighborhood stole wood sometimes from his pile; whereupon the Governor in a seeming anger did reply, "Does he so? I'll take a course with him; go, call that man to me; I'll warrant you I'll cure him of stealing!"

When the man came, the Governor, considering that if he had stolen, it was more out of necessity than disposition, said unto him: "Friend, it is a severe winter, and I doubt you are but meanly provided for wood; wherefore I would have you supply yourself at my woodpile till this cold season be over." And he then merrily asked his friends whether he had not effectually cured this man of stealing his wood?...

There was a time when he received a very sharp letter from a gentleman who was a member of the court, but he delivered back the letter unto the messengers that brought it with such a Christian speech as this: "I am not willing to keep such a matter of provocation by me!" Afterwards the same gentleman was compelled by the scarcity of provisions to send unto him that he would sell him some of his cattle; whereupon the Governor prayed him to accept what he had sent for as a token of his good will; but the gentleman returned him this answer: "Sir, your overcoming of yourself hath overcome me."

THE FIRST LETTER: BEFORE LEAVING ENGLAND

MY Faithful and Dear Wife,—It pleaseth God, that thou shouldst once again hear from me before our departure, and I hope this shall come safe to thy hands. I know it will be a great refreshing to thee. And blessed be His mercy, that I can write thee so good news, that we are all in very good health, and, having tried our ship's entertainment now more than a week, we find it agrees very well with us. Our boys are well and cheerful, and have no mind of home. They lie both with me, and sleep as soundly in a rug (for we use no sheets here) as ever they did at Groton; and so I do myself (I praise God).

The wind hath been against us this week and more; but this day it is come fair to the north, so as we are preparing (by God's assistance) to set sail in the morning. We have only four ships ready, and some two or three Hollanders go along with us. The rest of our fleet (being seven ships) will not be ready this sennight [for a week]. We have spent now two Sabbaths on shipboard very comfortably (God be praised) and are daily more and more encouraged to look for the Lord's presence to go along with us....

We are, in all our eleven ships, about seven hundred persons, passengers, and two hundred and forty cows, and about sixty horses. The ship, which went from Plymouth, carried about one hundred and forty persons, and the ship, which goes from Bristol, carrieth about eighty persons. And now (my sweet soul) I must once again take my last farewell of thee in Old England. It goeth very near my heart to leave thee; but I know to Whom I have committed thee, even to Him Who loves thee much better than any husband can, Who hath taken account of the hairs of thy head, and puts all thy tears in His bottle, Who can, and (if it be for His glory) will bring us together again with peace and comfort. Oh, how it refresheth my heart, to think, that I shall yet again see thy sweet face in the land of the living!—that lovely countenance that I have so much delighted in and beheld with so great content!

I have hitherto been so taken up with business, as I could seldom look back to my former happiness, but now when I shall be at some leisure, I shall not avoid the remembrance of thee, nor the grief for thy absence. Thou hast thy share with me, but I hope the course we have agreed upon will be some ease to us both. Mondays and Fridays, at five of the clock at night, we shall meet in spirit till we meet in person. Yet if all these hopes should fail, blessed be our God, that we are assured we shall meet one day, if not as husband and wife, yet in a better condition. Let that stay and comfort thy heart. Neither can the sea drown thy husband, nor enemies destroy, nor any adversity deprive thee of thy husband or children.

Therefore I will only take thee now and my sweet children in mine arms, and kiss and embrace you all, and so leave you with my God. Farewell, farewell. I bless you all in the name of the Lord Jesus. I salute my daughter Winth., Matt., Nan., and the rest, and all my good neighbors and friends. Pray all for us. Farewell. Commend my blessing to my son John. I cannot now write to him, but tell him I have committed thee and thine to him. Labor to draw him yet nearer to God, and he will be the surer staff of comfort to thee. I cannot name the rest of my good friends, but thou canst supply it. I wrote a week since to thee and Mr. Leigh and divers others.

Thine wheresoever,

Jo. Winthrop

From aboard the ARBELLA, riding at the COWES.
March 28, 1630

THE SECOND LETTER: FROM MASSACHUSETTS BAY

Charlestown in New England
July 16, 1630

MY DEAR WIFE,—Blessed be the Lord, our good God and merciful Father, that yet hath preserved me in life and health to salute thee, and to comfort thy long longing heart with the joyful news of my welfare, and the welfare of thy beloved children.

We had a long and troublesome passage, but the Lord made it safe and easy to us; and though we have met with many and great troubles (as this bearer can certify thee) yet He hath pleased to uphold us, and give us hope of a happy issue.

I am so overpressed with business, as I have no time for these or other mine own private occasions. I only write now that thou mayest know that yet I live and am mindful of thee in all my affairs. The larger discourse of all things thou shalt receive from my brother Downing, which I must send by some of the last ships. We have met with many sad and discomfortable things, as thou shalt hear after, and the Lord's hand hath been heavy upon myself in some very near to me. My son Henry! my son Henry! ah, poor child! [His son Henry was drowned on the day the ship landed.] Yet it grieves me much more for my dear daughter. The Lord strengthen and comfort her heart, to bear this cross patiently. I know thou wilt not be wanting to her in this distress. Yet for all these things (I praise my God) I am not discouraged; nor do I see cause to repent or despair of those good days here, which will make amends for all.

I shall expect thee next summer if the Lord please) and by that time I hope to be provided for thy comfortable entertainment. My most sweet wife, be not disheartened; trust in the Lord, and thou shalt see His faithfulness.

Commend me heartily to all our kind friends...and all the rest of my neighbors and their wives, both rich and poor....

The good Lord be with thee and bless thee and all our children and servants.

Commend my love to them all; I kiss and embrace thee, my dear wife, and all my children, and leave thee in His arms, Who is able to preserve you all, and to fulfill our joy in our happy meeting in His good time. Amen.

Thy faithful husband,

                Jo. Winthrop.

II. Religious Life in America

NEW ENGLAND

Religion played a vital role in the lives of our colonial ancestors. Massachusetts and Virginia began during an age when men were fighting religious wars in Europe. The Puritans came to America so that they could worship God in their own manner. Even the Virginians, who came for more worldly reasons, took their religion very seriously. Almost nowhere in the world in those days did people believe that religion was a private matter between man and God. The Puritans were extremely intolerant of other religions and persecuted Quakers, Catholics, and Jews alike. They even persecuted each other. Roger Williams, who founded Rhode Island, was banished from Massachusetts for his opinions, and innocent women were hanged in Salem because they were thought to be witches. The intolerance and persecution of the seventeenth century are well known, but one should not overlook the admirable piety and intense love of God that these people also had.

Edward Taylor 1645-1729

The following selections were written by Edward Taylor (1645-1729), the most important American poet of the Puritan period. He preached in a frontier town of western Massachusetts and wrote poetry privately to express his great love for God. Because his poems were so personal, he did not want them published, and they remained in manuscript for more than 200 years. Finally they were found in a dusty corner of the Yale University Library.

In the following poem, Taylor imagines himself in heaven looking down on his fellow New England Puritans, who are on their way to heaven in a horse-drawn coach—Christ's coach—which, of course, means figuratively that they are going to heaven through believing in Christ. These New England saints are singing at the top of their lungs, happy that they are in Christ's coach, but you will note that the harmony is not perfect. Man is a sinful creature and sometimes, says Taylor, the singers get out of tune. Also, he notes, there isn't room in the coach for everyone, and some have to walk.

The Joy of Church Fellowship Rightly Attended

>   IN heaven soaring up, I dropt an ear
>   On earth, and oh! sweet melody!
>   And listening, found it was the saints who were
>   Encoached for heaven that sang for joy.
>   For in Christ's coach they sweetly sing,
>   As they to glory ride therein.
>   Oh! joyous hearts! Enfired with holy flame!
>   Is speech thus tasseled with praise?
>   Will not your inward fire of joy contain
>   That it in open flames doth blaze?
>   For in Christ's coach saints sweetly sing,
>   As they to glory ride therein.
>   And if a string do slip, by chance, they soon
>   Do screw it up again: whereby
>   They set it in a more melodious tune
>   And a diviner harmony.
>   For in Christ's coach they sweetly sing,
>   As they to glory ride therein.

In all their acts, public and private, nay,
    And secret too, they praise impart.
But in their acts divine and worship, they
    With hymns do offer up their heart.
    Thus in Christ's coach they sweetly sing,
    As they to glory ride therein.
Some few not in, and some whose time and place
    Block up this coach's way, do go
As travelers afoot: and so do trace
    The road that gives them right thereto;
    While in this coach these sweetly sing,
    As they to glory ride therein.

Next, Taylor's great love of God is expressed in a beautiful figure of speech in which the poet wants God to use him as a housewife uses wool to make yarn and yarn to make cloth. In the first stanza, he asks God to make him into a spinning wheel, of which the flyers, distaff, spool, and reel all are parts. In the second stanza, Taylor wants to be a loom on which God can weave holy robes. A fulling mill is a place where cloth is dyed. Finally, the poet wants God to clothe him in the holy robes made on this imaginary loom. This poem is a highly original way to ask God to give one faith, love, and understanding. You should consider it a prayer.

Housewifery

    MAKE me, o Lord, Thy spinning-wheel complete;
    Thy holy Word my distaff make for me;
    Make mine affections Thy swift flyers neat;
    And make my soul Thy holy spool to be;
    My conversation make to be Thy reel,
    And reel the yarn thereon, spun of Thy wheel.
    Make me Thy loom then; knit therein this twine;

And make Thy Holy Spirit, Lord, wind quills;
Then weave the web Thyself. The yarn is fine.
Thine ordinances make my fulling mills.
Then dye the same in heavenly colors choice,
All pinked with varnished flowers of paradise.
Then clothe therewith mine understanding, will,
Affections, judgment, conscience, memory,
My words and actions, that their shine may fill
My ways with glory and Thee glorify.
Then mine apparel shall display before Ye
That I am clothed in holy robes for glory.

The Salem Witch Trials

During the seventeenth century, the superstitions of the Middle Ages had not yet relaxed their hold on men's minds. People still believed in witches, even such a prominent clergyman as Cotton Mather. Hence, the events of 1692 in Salem, Massachusetts, are understandable, though they are nonetheless tragic. Early that year Betty Parris and Abigail Williams, who were nine and eleven years old, began having strange fits. Soon the mysterious disease spread to other girls in the village. When the local doctor, with his primitive knowledge of medicine, could not diagnose the trouble, he concluded that the devil must have bewitched the girls.

This diagnosis did not surprise anyone. The New England Puritans believed that the devil was always at work trying to tempt them from the path of righteousness. The parents of the children set about to discover the identity of the devil's agent who was tormenting their girls. They questioned the children at length until the children really began to believe they were bewitched. Betty and Abigail then accused three women in the community of practicing witchcraft: Tituba, an illiterate slave from Barbados;

Sarah Good, a sharp-tongued woman whom many in the village thought a nuisance; and Sarah Osburne, a backslider who did not go to church. No one was surprised when these women were named as witches. The town proceeded to examine the three on charges of practicing witchcraft. John Hathorne, ancestor of the novelist Nathaniel Hawthorne, conducted the hearing in the village church.

The first of the accused to be questioned was Sarah Good, who denied the charges with vigor. Then came Sarah Osburne, who was dragged out of a sickbed to testify. She, too, denied the charges. But, every time these women denied the charges the children became hysterical and went into their fits. Finally, the old slave Tituba was questioned. She apparently decided that she should tell her accusers what they wanted to hear, and she concocted a wild tale of witchcraft out of her rich imagination. The selections that follow are actual transcripts of the testimony taken down that infamous day, March 1, 1692, in Salem by the village clerk. The proceedings have been edited just enough to make them readable.

HATHORNE: Sarah Good, what evil spirit have you familiarity with?
GOOD: None.
H: Have you made no contract with the devil?
G: No.
H: Why do you hurt these children?
G: I do not hurt them. I scorn it.
H: Who do you employ then to do it?
G: I employ nobody.
H: What creature do you employ then?
G: No creature; I am falsely accused.
H: Why did you go away muttering from Mr. Parris' house?
G: I did not mutter, but I thanked him for what he gave my child.

H: Have you made no contract with the devil?
G: No.

Judge Hathorne desired the children, all of them, to look upon her and see if this were the person that had hurt them, and so they all did look upon her and said this was one of the persons that did torment them. Presently they were all tormented.

H: Sarah Good, do you not see now what you have done? Why do you not tell us the truth? Why do you thus torment these poor children?
G: I do not torment them.
H: Who do you employ then?
G: I employ nobody. I scorn it.
H: How came they thus tormented?
G: What do I know? You bring others here, and now you charge me with it.
H: Why who was it?
G: I do not know, but it was someone you brought into the meeting house with you.
H: We brought you into the meeting house.
G: But you brought in two more.
H: Who was it then that tormented the children?
G: It was Osburne.
H: What is it you say when you go muttering away from persons' houses?
G: If I must tell, I will tell.
H: Do tell us then.
G: It is the commandments. I may say my commandments, I hope.

The testimony went on for a while longer. Sarah Good continued to be a very uncooperative witness, but finally Judge Hathorne finished with her and called Sarah Osburne to the stand.

HATHORNE: What evil spirit have you familiarity with?

OSBURNE: None.

H: Have you made no contract with the devil?

O: No, I never saw the devil in my life.

H: Why do you hurt these children?

O: I do not hurt them.

H: Who do you employ then to hurt them?

O: I employ nobody.

H: What familiarity have you with Sarah Good?

O: None. I have not seen her these two years.

H: Where did you see her then?

O: One day a-going to town.

H: What communications had you with her?

O: I had none, only, how do you do or so. I did not know her by name.

H: What did you call her then?

[At this point Sarah Osburne had to admit that she had called her Sarah.]

H: Sarah Good saith that it was you that hurt the children.

O: I do not know if the devil goes about in my likeness to do any hurt.

Mr. Hathorne desired all the children to stand up and look upon her and see if they did know her, which they all did, and every one of them said that this was one of the women that did afflict them and that they had constantly seen her in the very habit that she was now in.

The evidence continued. In a feeble effort to gain sympathy, she said that she "was more like to be bewitched than that she was a witch." Mr. Hathorne asked her what made her say this. She answered that she was frightened one time in her sleep and either saw or dreamed that she saw a thing "like an Indian all black which did prick her in the neck and pulled her by the back part of her head to the door of the house." Mr. Hathorne asked her if she had seen anything else. She replied that she had not. At this point, however, some of the spectators said that Sarah Osburne also had heard the voice of a lying spirit.

H: HATH the devil ever deceived you and been false to you?
O: I do not know the devil. I never did see him.
H: What lying spirit was it then?
O: It was a voice that I thought I heard.
H: What did it propound to you?
O: That I should go no more to meeting, but I said I would and did go the next Sabbath day.
H: Were you never tempted further?
O: No.
H: Why did you yield thus far to the devil as never to go to meeting since?
O: Alas! I have been sick and not able to go.

Sarah Osburne was then dismissed from the stand, and Mr. Hathorne began to question Tituba, the slave, who told her questioners just what they wanted to hear.

HATHORNE: Did you never see the devil?
TITUBA: The devil came to me and bid me serve him....
H: What service?
T: Hurt the children, and last night there was an appearance [apparition] that said to kill the children and if I would not go on hurting the children they would do worse to me.
H: What is this appearance you see?
T: Sometimes he is like a hog and sometimes like a great dog.
H: What did it say to you?
T: The black dog said, "Serve me," but I said, "I am afraid." He said if I did not he would do worse to me.
H: What did you say to it?
T: I will serve you no longer. Then he said he would hurt me, and

then he looked like a man. This man had a yellow bird that he kept with him, and he told me he had more pretty things that he would give me if I would serve him....

H: Did you not pinch Elizabeth Hubbard this morning?

T: The man brought her to me and made me pinch her.

H: Why did you go to Thomas Putnam's last night and hurt his child?

T: They pull and haul me and make me go....

H: How did you go?

T: We ride upon sticks and are there presently. H: Why did you not tell your master?

T: I was afraid. They said they would cut off my head if I told....

H: Did not you hurt Mr. Corwin's child?

T: Goody [Mrs.] Good and Goody Osburne told me that they did hurt Mr. Corwin's child and would have had me hurt him too, but I did not....

H: Do you see who it is that torments these children now?

T: Yes, it is Goody Good. She hurts them now in her own shape.

And so the testimony went. Tituba's story was even more sensational when she described the "tall man of Boston," who was supposed to be a wizard in charge of all the local witches. The court adjourned for the day, convinced that the devil had chosen Salem as a special point of attack. Soon, other people in the village began imagining that they, too, were being pursued by witches. Neighbor began accusing neighbor until the whole community was swept up by the hysteria.

Throughout the summer of 1692, Salem was gripped by the witch hunt. Twenty persons were executed for witchcraft; 55 were frightened or tortured into confessing their guilt; 150 were jailed; more than 200 were denounced by former friends and neighbors. For a time it looked as if Massachusetts had gone mad. But when the denunciations began to include some of the most prominent members of the community, such as the acting president of Harvard College, the authorities knew the hysteria had to stop or it would destroy the colony. In September the trials were halted and the jails emptied. In succeeding years many people repented their part in the tragic business, and the state even restored some of the property confiscated from the so-called witches.

Five years after the unhappy episode ended, one of the judges, Samuel Sewall, courageously made public confession of error. As the minister read aloud Sewall's confession of shame, the judge stood in his pew with head bowed.

"SAMUEL Sewall, sensible of the reiterated strokes of God upon himself and family, and being sensible that as to the guilt contracted upon the opening of the late commission of Oyer and Terminer at Salem [the trials], to which the order for this Day relates, he is, upon many accounts, more concerned than any that he knows of, desires to take the blame and shame of it, asking pardon of men and especially desiring prayers that God, Who has an unlimited authority, would pardon that sin and all other his sins, personal and relative: and according to His infinite benignity and sovereignty not visit the sin of him or of any other upon himself or any of his, nor upon the land: but that He would powerfully defend him against all temptations to sin for the future and vouchsafe him the efficacious saving conduct of His word and spirit."

Thereafter, for the rest of his life, Samuel Sewall observed one day of prayer and fasting each year as penance for his part in the Salem witch trials.

The Great Awakening

Within a century after the Puritan migration to New England, life in the colonies was changing. New England Puritans were becoming Yankee traders, and the religious fervor that brought

Bradford and Winthrop and their followers to the New World was dying out. At this time there appeared upon the American scene a great preacher and theologian, Jonathan Edwards. After entering Yale College at the age of 13, he had gone on to study theology and then enter the ministry. By 1729 he had succeeded his grandfather as pastor of the village church in Northampton, Massachusetts. During his ministry in Northampton, Edwards led a great revival movement, which has come to be known as the Great Awakening. It was an effort to rekindle the dying sparks of Puritanism, and for a time it brought new religious vitality to New England. The movement also spread to other colonies.

During the Great Awakening Edwards made many converts. While he was doing this, he also was concerned with the psychology of religious enthusiasm. One of his most interesting books is called *Narrative of Surprising Conversions*. In it he records some of the more remarkable effects of the revival movement that he led. The account of four-year-old Phebe Bartlet's conversion, which Edwards writes about in the following selection, is an astonishing story. Phebe certainly was not a typical child, but the fact that any child could undergo the religious experience Edwards describes reminds us again that religion played a central role in the lives of our colonial ancestors.

SHE was born in March, in the year 1731. About the latter end of April, or beginning of May, 1735, she was greatly affected by the talk of her brother, who had been hopefully converted a little before, at about eleven years of age, and then seriously talked to her about the great things of religion. Her parents did not know of it at that time, and were not wont, in the counsels they gave to their children, particularly to direct themselves to her, by reason of her being so young, and, as they supposed, not capable of understanding; but after her brother had talked to her, they observed her very earnestly to listen to the advice they gave to the other children, and she was observed very constantly to retire, several times in a day, as was concluded, for secret prayer, and grew more and more engaged in religion, and was more frequently in her closet, till at last she was wont to visit it five or six times in a day, and was so engaged in it, that nothing would, at any time, divert her from her stated closet exercises. Her mother often observed and watched her, when such things occurred, as she thought most likely to divert her, either by putting it out of her thoughts, or otherwise engaging her inclinations, but never could observe her to fail. She mentioned some very remarkable instances.

She once, of her own accord, spake of her unsuccessfulness, in that she could not find God, or to that purpose. But on Thursday, the last of July, about the middle of the day, the child being in the closet, where it used to retire, its mother heard it speaking aloud, which was unusual, and never had been observed before; and her voice seemed to be as of one exceeding importunate and engaged, but her mother could distinctly hear only these words (spoken in her childish manner, but seemed to be spoken with extraordinary earnestness, and out of distress of soul), "Pray BLESSED LORD, give me salvation! I PRAY, BEG, pardon all my sins!" When the child had done prayer, she came out of the closet, and came and sat down by her mother, and cried out aloud. Her mother very earnestly asked her several times, what the matter was, before she would make any answer, but she continued exceedingly crying, and wreathing her body to and fro, like one in anguish of spirit. Her mother then asked her whether she was afraid that God would not give her salvation. She then answered, "Yes, I am afraid I shall go to hell!" Her mother then endeavored to quiet her, and told her she would not have her cry—she must be a good girl, and pray every day, and she hoped God would give her salvation. But this did not quiet her at all—but she continued thus earnestly crying and taking on for some time, till at length she suddenly ceased crying and began to smile, and presently said with a smiling countenance, "Mother, the kingdom of heaven is come to me!" Her mother was surprised at the sudden alteration, and at the speech, and knew not what to make of it, but at first said nothing to her....

The same day the elder children, when they came home from school, seemed much affected with the extraordinary change that seemed to be made in Phebe; and her sister Abigail standing by, her mother took occasion to counsel her, now to improve her time, to prepare for another world; on which Phebe burst out in tears, and cried out, "Poor Nabby!" Her mother told her she would not have her cry, she hoped that God would give Nabby salvation; but that did not quiet her, but she continued earnestly crying for some time; and when she had in a measure ceased, her sister Eunice being by her, she burst out again, and cried, "Poor Eunice!" and cried exceedingly; and when she had almost done, she went into another room, and there looked upon her sister Naomi, and burst out again, crying, "Poor Amy!" Her mother was greatly affected at such behavior in the child, and knew not what to say to her. One of the neighbors coming in a little after, asked her what she had cried for., She seemed, at first, backward to tell the reason. Her mother told her she might tell that person, for he had given her an apple; upon which she said she cried because she was afraid they would go to hell....

From this time there has appeared a very remarkable abiding change in the child: she has been very strict upon the Sabbath, and seems to long for the Sabbath day before it comes, and will often in the week time be inquiring how long it is to the Sabbath day, and must have the days particularly counted over that are between, before she will be contented. And she seems to love God's house —is very eager to go thither. Her mother once asked her why she had such a mind to go? Whether it was not to see the fine folks? She said no, it was to hear Mr. Edwards preach. When she is in the place of worship, she is very far from spending her time there as children at her age usually do, but appears with an attention that is very extraordinary for such a child. She also appears, very desirous at all opportunities, to go to private religious meetings, and is very still and attentive at home, in prayer time, and has appeared affected in time of family prayer.

OTHER COLONIES

Although one may think first of New England Puritanism in discussing the religious life of the colonies, America was founded by many religious groups. The Church of England was dominant in the southern colonies, Maryland was founded by Catholics, and New York was settled by Netherlanders who belonged to the Dutch Reformed Church. Still another important religious influence was the Quaker faith, represented most significantly by William Penn, who established the Pennsylvania colony. There also were many Quakers in New Jersey, one of whom, John Woolman, is the writer of the following selection.

Woolman was a simple, plain tailor and shopkeeper who spent much of his adult life traveling about the colonies visiting Quaker churches. His Journal gives a clear account of the faith and life of a Quaker. The portion printed below (from the original edition published in Philadelphia in 1774) details Woolman's boyhood and early religious experience.

I WAS born in Northampton, in Burlington County, West Jersey, in the year 1720; and before I was seven years old I began to be acquainted with the operations of divine love. Through the care of my parents, I was taught to read nearly as soon as I was capable of it; and, as I went from school one Seventh Day [the Quaker's term for Saturday; Sunday is the First Day], I remember, while my companions went to play by the way, I went forward out of sight, and, sitting down, I read the 22d Chapter of the Revelations: "He showed me a pure river of water of life, clear as crystal, proceeding out of the throne of God and of the Lamb," etc., and, in reading it, my mind was drawn to seek after that pure habitation, which, I then believed, God had prepared for His servants. The place where I sat, and the sweetness that attended my mind, remain fresh in my memory.

This, and the like gracious visitations, had that effect upon me, that when boys used ill language it troubled me; and, through the continued mercies of God, I was preserved from it.

The pious instructions of my parents were often fresh in my mind when I happened to be among wicked children, and were of use to me. My parents, having a large family of children, used frequently, on First Days after meeting, to put us to read in the holy scriptures, or some religious books, one after another, the rest sitting by without much conversation; which, I have since often thought, was a good practice. From what I had read and heard, I believed there had been, in past ages, people who walked in uprightness before God, in a degree exceeding any that I knew, or heard of, now living: and the apprehension of there being less steadiness and firmness, amongst people in this age than in past ages, often troubled me while I was a child....

A thing remarkable in my childhood was, that once, going to a neighbour's house, I saw, on the way, a robin sitting on her nest, and as I came near she went off, but having young ones flew about, and with many cries expressed her concern for them; I stood and threw stones at her, till, one striking her, she fell down dead: at first I was pleased with the exploit, but after a few minutes was seized with horror, as having, in a sportive way, killed an innocent creature while she was careful for her young. I beheld her lying dead, and thought these young ones, for which she was so careful, must now perish for want of their dam to nourish them; and after some painful considerations on the subject, I climbed up the tree, took all the young birds, and killed them; supposing that better than to leave them to pine away and die miserably: and believed, in this case, that scripture-proverb was fulfilled, "The tender mercies of the wicked are cruel." I then went on my errand, but, for some hours, could think of little else but the cruelties I had committed, and was much troubled. Thus, He,

Whose tender mercies are over all His works, hath placed a principle in the human mind, which incites to exercise goodness towards every living creature; and this being singly attended to, people become tender hearted and sympathizing; but being frequently and totally rejected, the mind becomes shut up in a contrary disposition.

About the twelfth year of my age, my father being abroad, my mother reproved me for some misconduct, to which I made an undutiful reply; and, the next First Day, as I was with my father returning from meeting, he told me he understood I had behaved amiss to my mother, and advised me to be more careful in [the] future. I knew myself blameable, and in shame and confusion remained silent. Being thus awakened to a sense of my wickedness, I felt remorse in my mind, and, getting home, I retired and prayed to the Lord to forgive me; and do not remember that I ever, after that, spoke unhandsomely to either of my parents, however foolish in some other things.

Having attained the age of sixteen years, I began to love wanton company; and though I was preserved from profane language, or scandalous conduct, still I perceived a plant in me which produced much wild grapes; yet my merciful Father forsook me not utterly, but, at times, through His grace, I was brought seriously to consider my ways; and the sight of my backslidings affected me with sorrow; but, for want of rightly attending to the reproofs of instruction, vanity was added to vanity, and repentance to repentance: upon the whole, my mind was more and more alienated from the truth, and I hastened toward destruction. While I meditate on the gulf towards which I travelled, and reflect on my youthful disobedience, for these things I weep, mine eyes run down with water.

Advancing in age, the number of my acquaintances increased, and thereby my way grew more difficult; though I had found comfort in reading the holy scriptures, and thinking on heavenly things, I was now estranged therefrom: I knew I was going from the flock of Christ, and had no resolution to return; hence serious reflections were uneasy to me, and youthful vanities and diversions my greatest pleasure. Running in this road I found many like myself; and we associated in that which is the reverse of true friendship.

But in this swift race it pleased God to visit me with sickness, so that I doubted of recovering; and then did darkness, horror, and amazement, with full force, seize me, even when my pain and distress of body was very great. I thought it would have been better for me never to have had a being, than to see the day which I now saw. I was filled with confusion; and in great affliction, both of mind and body, I lay and bewailed myself. I had not confidence to lift up my cries to God, Whom I had thus offended; but, in a deep sense of my great folly, I was humbled before Him; and, at length, that Word which is as a fire and a hammer, broke and dissolved my rebellious heart, and then my cries were put up in contrition; and in the multitude of His mercies I found inward relief, and felt a close engagement, that, if He was pleased to restore my health, I might walk humbly before Him.

III. Colonial Problems

INDIAN TROUBLES

As we have seen, the task of planting colonies in the New World took stout hearts and strong arms. The major problem was the unspectacular one of scratching a living from the soil. There were, in addition, more dramatic problems, such as Indian skirmishes and even full-scale war. More and more land was being taken up by the English settlers. In New England, an Indian leader known as King Philip organized a big Indian drive to rid the country of English settlers. This drive was known as King Philip's War and was waged in the years 1675-76. In this conflict, the Indians of Massachusetts, Rhode Island, and Connecticut spread terror throughout New England and burnt many houses, but in the end were nearly wiped out themselves. During the next century, England and France fought for control of the Mississippi Valley. In the latter part of this struggle, between 1754 and 1763, usually called the French and Indian War, the American colonies found themselves the battleground for the rivalries of two great European powers.

Mrs. Rowlandson's Captivity

In the selection that follows, Mary Rowlandson, a New England housewife, tells of her capture by the Indians and her captivity during King Philip's War. She was held by the Indians for twelve weeks until her friends were able to ransom her. As vivid today as when it was written in 1682, this narrative is called *A True History of the Captivity and Restoration of Mrs. Mary Rowlandson*.

THE ATTACK

ON the tenth of February, 1675, came the Indians with great numbers upon Lancaster [Massachusetts]. Their first coming was about sunrising; hearing the noise of some guns, we looked out; several houses were burning, and the smoke ascending to heaven. There were five persons taken in one house; the father and the mother and a sucking child they knocked on the head; the other two they took and carried away alive. There were two others who, being out of their garrison upon some occasion, were set upon; one was knocked on the head, the other escaped. Another there was who, running along, was shot and wounded, and fell down; he begged of them his life, promising them money (as they told me); but they would not hearken to him, but knocked him in [the] head, and stripped him naked, and split open his bowels. Another seeing many of the Indians about his barn ventured and went out, but was quickly shot down. There were three others belonging to the same garrison who were killed; the Indians, getting up upon the roof of the barn, had advantage to shoot down upon them over their fortification. Thus these murderous wretches went on, burning and destroying before them.

At length they came and beset our own house, and quickly it was the dolefulest day that ever mine eyes saw. The house stood upon the edge of a hill; some of the Indians got behind the hill, others into the barn, and others behind anything that could shelter them; from all which places they shot against the house, so that the bullets seemed to fly like hail; and quickly they wounded one man among us, then another, and then a third. About two hours (according to my observation in that. amazing time) they had been about the house before they prevailed to fire it (which they did with flax and hemp, which they brought out of the barn, and there being no defense about the house, only two flankers [fortifications] at two opposite corners, and one of them not finished). They fired it once and one ventured out and quenched it, but they quickly fired it again, and that took.

Now is the dreadful hour come that I have often heard of (in time of war, as it was in the case of others), but now mine eyes see it. Some in our house were fighting for their lives, others wallowing in their blood, the house on fire over our heads, and the bloody heathen ready to knock us on the head if we stirred out. Now might we hear mothers and children crying out for themselves and one another, "Lord, what shall we do?" Then I took my children (and one of my sisters hers) to go forth and leave the house, but as soon as we came to the door and appeared, the Indians shot so thick that the bullets rattled against the house as if one had taken an handful of stones and threw them, so that we were fain to give back. We had six stout dogs belonging to our garrison, but none of them would stir, though another time, if an Indian had come to the door, they were ready to fly upon him and tear him down. The Lord hereby would make us the more to acknowledge His hand, and to see that our help is always in Him.

But out we must go, the fire increasing, and coming along behind us roaring, and the Indians gaping before us with their guns, spears, and hatchets to devour us. No sooner were we out of the house but my brother-in-law (being before wounded in defending the house, in or near the throat) fell down dead, whereat the Indians scornfully shouted and hallowed, and were presently upon him, stripping off his clothes. The bullets flying thick, one went through my side, and the same (as would seem) through the bowels and hand of my dear child in my arms. One of my elder sister's children (named William) had then his leg broken, which the Indians perceiving they knocked him on the head. Thus were we butchered by those merciless heathen, standing amazed, with the blood running down to our heels. My eldest sister being yet in the house, and seeing those woeful sights, the infidels hauling mothers one way and children another, and some wallowing in their blood, and her elder son telling her that her son William was dead and myself was wounded, she said, "And, Lord, let me die with them"; which was no sooner said but she was struck with a bullet and fell down dead over the threshold.

> Of the thirty-seven persons in the house, twelve were killed and only one escaped. Mrs. Rowlandson and her baby were among the remaining twenty-four taken captive.

THE FIRST REMOVE

Now away we must go with those barbarous creatures, with our bodies wounded and bleeding, and our hearts no less than our bodies. About a mile we went that night up upon a hill, within sight of the town, where they intended to lodge. There was hard by a vacant house (deserted by the English before, for fear of the Indians); I asked them whether I might not lodge in the house that night, to which they answered, "What, will you love Englishmen still?" This was the dolefulest night that ever my eyes saw. Oh, the roaring, and singing, and dancing, and yelling of those black creatures in the night, which made the place a lively resemblance of hell! And as miserable was the waste that was there made, of horses, cattle, sheep, swine, calves, lambs, roasting pigs, and fowl (which they had plundered in the town), some roasting, some lying and burning, and some boiling, to feed our merciless enemies, who were joyful enough, though we were disconsolate.

To add to the dolefulness of the former day and the dismalness of the present night, my thoughts ran upon my losses and sad, bereaved condition. All was gone, my husband gone (at least separated from me, he being in the Bay; and to add to my grief, the Indians told me they would kill him as he came homeward), my children gone, my relations and friends gone, our house and home, and all our comforts within door and without—all was gone (except my life), and I knew not but the next moment that might go too.

There remained nothing to me but one poor, wounded babe, and it seemed at present worse than death, that it was in such a pitiful condition, bespeaking compassion, and I had no refreshing for it nor suitable things to revive it. Little do many think what is the savageness and brutishness of this barbarous enemy...when the English have fallen into their hands....

THE SECOND REMOVE

But now (the next morning) I must turn my back upon the town, and travel with them into the vast and desolate wilderness, I know not whither. It is not my tongue or pen can express the sorrows of my heart and bitterness of my spirit that I had at this departure; but God was with me in a wonderful manner, carrying me along and bearing up my spirit, that it did not quite fail. One of the Indians carried my poor wounded babe upon a horse; it went moaning all along: "I shall die, I shall die." I went on foot after it, with sorrow that cannot be expressed. At length I took it off the horse and carried it in my arms, till my strength failed and I fell down with it.

Then they set me upon a horse with my wounded child in my lap; and there being no furniture [saddle] upon the horseback, as we were going down a steep hill, we both fell over the horse's head, at which they, like inhuman creatures, laughed and rejoiced to see it, though I thought we should there have ended our days, overcome with so many difficulties. But the Lord renewed my strength still, and carried me along, that I might see more of His power, yea, so much that I could never have thought of, had I not experienced it.

After this it quickly began to snow; and when the night came on they stopped; and now down I must sit in the snow by a little fire, and a few boughs behind me, with my sick child in my lap and calling much for water, being now (through the wound) fallen into a violent fever. My own wound also growing so stiff that I could scarce sit down or rise up, yet so it must be, that I must sit all this cold winter night upon the cold snowy ground, with my sick child in my arms, looking that every hour would be the last of its life, and having no Christian friend near me, either to comfort or help me. Oh, I may see the wonderful power of God, that my spirit did not utterly sink under my affliction; still the Lord upheld me with His gracious and merciful spirit, and we were both alive to see the light of the next morning.

THE THIRD REMOVE

The morning being come, they prepared to go on their way. One of the Indians got up upon a horse, and they set me up behind him, with my poor sick babe in my lap. A very wearisome and tedious day I had of it; what with my own wound and my child's being so exceeding sick, and in a lamentable condition with her wound. It may be easily judged what a poor feeble condition we were in, there being not the least crumb of refreshing that came within either of our mouths from Wednesday night to Saturday night, except only a little cold water....

Thus nine days I sat upon my knees with my babe in my lap, till my flesh was raw again; my child being even ready to depart this sorrowful world, they bade me carry it out to another wigwam (I suppose because they would not be troubled with such spectacles) whither I went with a very heavy heart, and down I sat with the picture of death in my lap. About two hours in the night my sweet babe like a lamb departed this life, on February 18, 1675, it being about six years and five months old. It was nine days from the first wounding, in this miserable condition, without any refreshing of one nature or other, except a little cold water....In the morning, when they understood that my child was dead they sent for me home to my master's wigwam....I went to take up my dead child in my arms to carry it with me, but they bid me let it alone. There was no resisting, but go I must and leave it. When I had been at my master's wigwam, I took the first opportunity I could get to go look after my dead child. When I came I asked them what they had done with it? Then they told me it was upon the hill. Then they went and showed me where it was, where I saw the ground was newly digged, and there they told me they had buried it. There I left that child in the wilderness and must commit it and myself also in this wilderness condition to Him who is above all.

> Mrs. Rowlandson's ordeal lasted twelve weeks, after which she was ransomed and allowed to return home to her husband, who had survived the attack. Her two other children, also captured with her, were rescued and reunited with their parents.

CONFLICT WITH FRANCE

On July 9, 1755, during the French and Indian War, Colonel George Washington took part in the Battle of Monongahela, in which General Braddock was killed and his army routed. Washington had advised Braddock to push on rapidly towards the French-held Fort Duquesne and to leave behind his artillery and baggage wagons so that he could move through the wilderness as fast as possible. Washington feared the consequences of moving too slowly and wrote his brother a few days before the battle that the army "instead of pushing on with vigor, without regarding a little rough road" was "halting to level every mold hill and to erect bridges over every brook; by which means we were four days getting twelve miles." Washington's fear of disaster was only too well-founded. The following letter is his account of the battle, written to his mother nine days later:

Fort Cumberland, July 18, 1755

Honored Madam:

As I doubt not but you have heard of our defeat, and perhaps have it represented in a worse light (if possible) than it deserves; I have taken this earliest opportunity to give you some account of the engagement, as it happened within seven miles of the French fort, on Wednesday the ninth.

We marched on to that place without any considerable loss, having only now and then a straggler picked up by the French scouting Indians. When we came here, we were attacked by a body of French and Indians whose number (I am certain) did not exceed 300 men; ours consisted of about 1,300 well-armed troops, chiefly of the English soldiers who were struck with such a panic that they behaved with more cowardice than it is possible to conceive. The officers behaved gallantly in order to encourage their men, for which they suffered greatly, there being nearly 60 killed and wounded, a large proportion out of the number we had! The Virginia troops showed a good deal of bravery and were near all killed, for I believe out of three companies that were there, there is scarce 30 men left alive. Capt. Peyrouny and all his officers down to a corporal was killed. Capt. Polson shared near as hard a fate, for only one of his was left. In short the dastardly behavior of those they call regulars exposed all others that were inclined to do their duty to almost certain death, and at last, in despite of all the efforts of the officers to the contrary, they broke and run as sheep pursued by dogs, and it was impossible to rally them.

The general was wounded, of which he died three days after. Sir Peter Halket was killed in the field where died many other brave officers. I luckily escaped without a wound, though I had four bullets through my coat and two horses shot under me. Captains Orme and Morris, two of the general's aides de camp, were wounded early in the engagement, which rendered the duty hard upon me, as I was the only person then left to distribute the general's orders, which I was scarcely able to do, as I was not half recovered from a violent illness that confined me to my bed and a wagon for above ten days. I am still in a weak and feeble condition, which induces me to halt here two or three days in hopes of recovering a little strength to enable me to proceed homewards, from whence, I fear, I shall not be able to stir till towards September, so that I shall not have the pleasure of seeing you till then, unless it be in Fairfax. Please give my love to Mr. Lewis [his brother-in-law] and my sister and compliments to Mr. Jackson and all other friends that inquire after me. I am, Honored Madam, your most dutiful son.

Benjamin Franklin shared George Washington's doubts about Braddock's ability to capture Fort Duquesne. As a public-spirited citizen, Franklin had taken the initiative in collecting wagons from Pennsylvania farmers to transport the army's supplies. His comments on Braddock, written many years later, come from his autobiography.

THIS general was, I think, a brave man, and might probably have made a figure as a good officer in some European war. But he had too much self-confidence, too high an opinion of the validity of regular troops, and too mean a one of both Americans and Indians. George Croghan, our Indian interpreter, joined him on his march with one hundred of those people, who might have been of great use to his army as guides, scouts, etc., if he had treated them kindly; but he slighted and neglected them, and they gradually left him.

In conversation with him one day, he was giving me some account of his intended progress. "After taking Fort Duquesne," says he, "I am to proceed to Niagara; and having taken that to Frontenac, if the season will allow time; and I suppose it will, for Duquesne can hardly detain me above three or four days; and then I see nothing that can obstruct my march to Niagara." Having before revolved in my mind the long line his army must make in their march by a very narrow road, to be cut for them through the woods and bushes, and also what I had read of a former defeat of fifteen hundred French who invaded the Iroquois country, I had conceived some doubts and Nome fears for the event of the campaign. But I ventured only to say, "To be sure, sir, if you arrive well before Duquesne, with these fine troops, so well provided with artillery, that place, not yet completely fortified, and as we hear with no very strong garrison, can probably make but a short resistance. The only danger I apprehend of obstruction to your march is from ambuscades of Indians, who, by constant practice, are dexterous in laying and executing them; and the slender line, near four miles long, which your army must make, may expose it to be attacked by surprise in its flanks, and to be cut like a thread into several pieces, which, from their distance, can not come up in time to support each other."

He smiled at my ignorance, and replied, "These savages may, indeed, be a formidable enemy to your raw American militia, but upon the king's regular and disciplined troops, sir, it is impossible they should make any impression." I was conscious of an impropriety in my disputing with a military man in matters of his profession, and said no more.

IV. Colonial Life

TRANSPORTATION

Life in the United States has changed beyond recognition from life in America in the seventeenth and eighteenth centuries. In thousands of ways people live differently. They work, they play, they eat, and they even sleep differently. Then, there was no station wagon in the garage to take the family to the beach or mountains over weekends and no telephone at hand to call a friend to ask how to do tomorrow's algebra problem. Life was slower-paced than it is today, and was not complicated by the machines that have become masters as well as slaves of our society. The selections that follow will give you an insight into the daily lives of several interesting early Americans. It is just as important to understand how people lived in colonial times as it is to know about wars and kings and presidents.

Sarah Kemble Knight 1666-1727

Madam Knight, as Sarah Kemble Knight is known, was a Boston schoolteacher and businesswoman. In the autumn of 1704 she made a business trip to New York by way of Rhode Island and Connecticut. On the journey she kept a journal which gives a vivid account of her experiences. You will find that this Boston woman writes about Connecticut as though it were a foreign country. She had a good sense of humor and a keen eye for detail. You learn in this report that not all of your New England ancestors were cultivated people like governors Winthrop and Bradford.

THE THIRD DAY

Wednesday, October 4, 1704

ABOUT four in the morning, we set out for Kingston [Rhode Island] (for so was the town called) with a French doctor in our company. He and the post put on very furiously, so that I could not keep up with them, only as now and then they'd stop till they see me. This road was poorly furnished with accommodations for travelers, so that we were forced to ride 22 miles by the post's account, but nearer thirty by mine, before we could bait [feed] so much as our horses, which I exceedingly complained of. But the post encouraged me by saying we should be well accommodated anon at Mr. Devil's, a few miles further. But I questioned whether we ought to go to the devil to be helped out of affliction. However, like the rest of [the] deluded souls that post to the infernal den, we made all possible speed to this devil's habitation, where alighting in full assurance of good accommodation, we were going in. But meeting his two daughters, as I supposed twins, they so nearly resembled each other, both in features and habit, and looked as old as the devil himself and quite as ugly, we desired entertainment but could hardly get a word out of 'em, till with our importunity [urging], telling them our necessity, etc., they called the old sophister, who was as sparing of his words as his daughters had been, and no, or none, was the reply he made us to our demands. He differed only in this from the old fellow in t'other country: he let us depart....

Thus leaving this habitation of cruelty, we went forward, and arriving at an ordinary [inn] about two mile further, found tolerable accommodation. But our hostess, being a pretty full-mouthed old creature, entertained our fellow traveler, the French doctor, with innumerable complaints of her bodily infirmities and whispered to him so loud that all the house had as full a hearing as he, which was very diverting to the company (of which there was a great many), as one might see by their sneering. But poor weary I slipped out to enter my mind in my journal, and left my great landlady with her talkative guests to themselves....

THE SIXTH DAY

Saturday, October 7

About two o'clock [in the] afternoon we arrived at New Haven [Connecticut], where I was received with all possible respects and civility. Here I discharged Mr. Wheeler with a reward to his satisfaction and took some time to rest after so long and toilsome a journey, and informed myself of the manners and customs of the place, and at the same time employed myself in the affair I went there upon.

They are governed by the same laws as we in Boston (or little differing) throughout this whole colony of Connecticut, and much the same way of church government and many of them good, sociable people, and I hope religious too. But [they are] a little too much independent in their principles, and, as I have been told, were formerly in their zeal very rigid in their administrations towards such as their laws made offenders, even to a harmless kiss or innocent merriment among young people....

Their diversions in this part of the country are on lecture days and [militia] training days mostly. On the former there is riding from town to town.

And on training days the youth divert themselves by shooting at the target, as they call it (but it very much resembles a pillory), where he that hits nearest the white has some yards of red ribbon presented him, which being tied to his hatband, the two ends streaming down his back, he is led away in triumph, with great applause, as the winners of the Olympic Games. They generally marry very young, the males oftener, as I am told, under twenty than above. They generally make public weddings and have a way something singular (as they say) in some of them, namely, just before joining hands the bridegroom quits the place, who is soon followed by the bridesmen, and as it were, dragged back to duty-being the reverse to the former practice among us, to steal his bride....

Being at a merchant's house, in comes a tall country fellow, with his alfogeos [cheeks] full of tobacco, for they seldom lose their cud but keep chewing and spitting as long as their eyes are open. He advanced to the middle of the room, makes an awkward nod, and spitting a large deal of aromatic tincture, he gave a scrape with his shovel-like shoe, leaving a small shovel full of dirt on the floor, made a full stop. Hugging his own pretty body with his hands under his arms, [he] stood staring round him like a cat let out of a basket. At last, like the creature Balaam rode on [an ass], he opened his mouth and said: "Have you any ribbon for hatbands to sell, I pray?" The questions and answers about the pay being past, the ribbon is brought and opened. Bumpkin Simpers cries, "It's confounded gay, I vow," and beckoning to the door, in comes Joan Tawdry, dropping about 50 curtsies, and stands by him. He shows her the ribbon. "Law you," says she, "It's right gent; do you take it; 'tis dreadful pretty." Then she inquires: "Have you any hood silk, I pray?" which being brought and bought, "Have you any thread silk to sew it with," says she, which being accommodated with, they departed. They generally stand, after they come in, a great while speechless and sometimes don't say a word till they are asked what they want, which I impute to the awe they stand in of the merchants, who they are constantly almost indebted to and must take what they bring without liberty to choose for themselves; but they serve them as well, making the merchants stay [wait] long enough for their pay.

LIFE IN THE SOUTH

A century after Jamestown was founded, Virginia was a prosperous, flourishing colony. The capital was moved a few miles away to Williamsburg, which today has been rebuilt to look much as it did in colonial times. Along the James River were large plantations, operated by gentleman farmers. These men lived much as their land-owning cousins did in the old country. Lower on the social scale, of course, were white indentured servants, who had bound themselves to years of labor in return for their passage to Virginia, and slaves.

William Byrd 1674-1744

The culture of the colony, however, was dominated by prosperous planters like William Byrd, ancestor of the present Byrd family of Virginia. His estate occupied the present site of Richmond. He was educated in England and active in the affairs of the colony.

In 1728, he was appointed to help survey the boundary between North Carolina and Virginia. The boundary, which was disputed, ran through virgin forests and over mountains. During the arduous weeks that the commissioners were making their survey, Byrd kept notes. His account of this experience is given in The History of the Dividing Line. You can see that Virginia gentlemen did not think much of the poor farmers in North Carolina.

LIFE IN NORTH CAROLINA

MARCH 25, 1728: Surely there is no place in the world where the inhabitants live with less labor than in North Carolina. It approaches nearer to the description of Lubberland [a mythical land of plenty and idleness] than any other, by the great felicity of the climate, the easiness of raising provisions, and the slothfulness of the people.

Indian corn is of so great increase that a little pains will subsist a very large family with bread, and then they may have meat without any pains at all, by the help of the low grounds, and the great variety of mast [nuts] that grows on the high land. The men, for their parts, just like the Indians, impose all the work upon the poor women. They make their wives rise out of their beds early in the morning, at the same time that they lie and snore till the sun has run one-third of his course and dispersed all the unwholesome damps. Then, after stretching and yawning for half an hour, they light their pipes, and, under the protection of a cloud of smoke, venture out into the open air, though if it happens to be never so little cold, they quickly return shivering into the chimney corner. When the weather is mild, they stand leaning with both their arms upon the cornfield fence, and gravely consider whether they had best go and take a small heat at the hoe, but generally find reasons to put it off till another time. Thus they loiter away their lives....

March 27: Within 3 or 4 miles of Edenton [North Carolina], the soil appears to be a little more fertile, though it is much cut with slashes [swamps], which seem all to have a tendency towards the Dismal.

This town is situate on the north side of Albemarle Sound, which is there about 5 miles over. A dirty slash runs all along the back of it, which in the summer is a foul annoyance and furnishes abundance of that Carolina plague, mosquitoes. There may be 40 or 50 houses, most of them small and built without expense. A citizen here is counted extravagant, if he has ambition enough to aspire to a brick chimney. Justice herself is but indifferently lodged, the court house having much the air of a common tobacco house. I believe this is the only metropolis in the Christian or Mohammedan world, where there is neither church, chapel, mosque, synagogue, or any other place of public worship of any sect or religion whatsoever.

What little devotion there may happen to be is much more private than their vices. The people seem easy without a minister, as long as they are exempted from paying him. Sometimes the society for propagating the Gospel has had the charity to send over missionaries to this country; but unfortunately the priest has been too lewd [worthless] for the people, or, which oftener happens, they too lewd for the priest. For these reasons these reverend gentlemen have always left their flocks as arrant heathen as they found them. Thus much, however, may be said for the inhabitants of Edenton, that not a soul has the least taint of hypocrisy or superstition, acting very frankly and aboveboard in all their excesses.

Provisions here are extremely cheap and extremely good, so that people may live plentifully at a trifling expense. Nothing is dear but law, physic, and strong drink, which are all bad in their kind, and the last they get with so much difficulty, that they are never guilty of the sin of suffering it to sour upon their hands. Their vanity generally lies not so much in having a handsome dining room as a handsome house of office [kitchen]. In this kind of structure they are really extravagant.

They are rarely guilty of flattering or making any court to their governors, but treat them with all the excesses of freedom and familiarity. They are of opinion their rulers would be apt to grow insolent, if they grew rich, and for that reason take care to keep them poorer, and more dependent, if possible, than the saints in New England used to do their governors.

> A Virginia planter had many responsibilities and many interests. Besides growing tobacco and raising livestock, Byrd and his associates made their plantations as self-sufficient as possible. Late in his life Byrd visited some mining property he owned in western Virginia, and on the trip stopped off to see Colonel Spotswood, a former governor of Virginia. The following account, from A Progress to the Mines, gives us a glimpse of another Virginian's house. Note, too, how Byrd concerns himself with collecting medicinal herbs.

A VISIT TO COLONEL SPOTSWOOD

SEPTEMBER 27, 1732: I came into the main county road that leads from Fredericksburg to Germanna, which last place I reached in ten miles more. This famous town consists of Col. Spotswood's enchanted castle on one side of the street and a baker's dozen of ruinous tenements on the other....Here I arrived about three o'clock and found only Mrs. Spotswood at home, who received her old acquaintance with many a gracious smile. I was carried into a room elegantly set off with pier glasses [full-length mirrors set between windows] the largest of which came soon after to an odd misfortune.

Amongst other favorite animals that cheered this lady's solitude, a brace of tame deer ran familiarly about the house, and one of them came to stare at me as a stranger. But unluckily spying his own figure in the glass, he made a spring over the tea table that stood under it, and shattered the glass to pieces, and falling back upon the tea table, made a terrible fracas among the china. This exploit was so sudden and accompanied with such a noise that it surprised me, and perfectly frightened Mrs. Spotswood. But 'twas worth all the damage to show the moderation and good humor with which she bore this disaster.

In the evening the noble colonel came home from his mines, who saluted me very civilly, and Mrs. Spotswood's sister, Miss Theky, who had been to meet him *en cavalier* [on horseback] was so kind too as to bid me welcome. We talked over a legend [collection] of old stories, supped about 9, and then prattled with the ladies till 'twas time for a traveler to retire. In the meantime I observed my old friend to be very uxorious [submissive to his wife] and exceedingly fond of his children. This was so opposite to the maxims he used to preach up before he was married, that I could not forbear rubbing up the memory of them. But he gave a very goodnatured turn to his change of sentiments by alleging that whoever brings a poor gentlewoman into so solitary a place, from all her friends and acquaintance, would be ungrateful not to use her and all that belongs to her with all possible tenderness.

September 28: We all kept snug in our several apartments till nine, except Miss Theky, who was the housewife of the family. At that hour we met over a pot of coffee, which was not quite strong enough to give us the palsy. After breakfast the Colonel and I left the ladies to their domestic affairs and took a turn in the garden, which has nothing beautiful but 3 terrace walks that fall in slopes one below another. I let him understand that besides the pleasure of paying him a visit, I came to be instructed by so great a master in the mystery of making of iron, wherein he had led the way....

September 30: The sun rose clear this morning, and so did I and finished all my little affairs by breakfast. It was then resolved to wait on the ladies on horseback, since the bright sun, the fine air, and the wholesome exercise all invited us to it. We forded the river a little above the ferry and rode 6 miles up the neck to a fine level piece of rich land where we found about 20 plants of ginseng, with the scarlet berries growing on the top of the middle stalk. The root of this is of wonderful virtue in many cases, particularly to raise the spirits and promote perspiration, which makes it a specific in colds and coughs. The colonel complimented me with all we found in return for my telling him the virtues of it. We were all pleased to find so much of this king of plants so near the colonel's habitation and growing too upon his own land....I carried home this treasure with as much joy as if every root had been a graft of the Tree of Life, and washed and dried it carefully.

LIFE IN A CITY

Benjamin Franklin's life is too well-known to need summarizing here. The story of his life should be on the reading list of every American, and the best account of it is the one he wrote himself. Unfortunately, he never finished his autobiography, so we do not have in his own words the story of his diplomatic mission to France during the Revolution, or his activities in America at the time of the Declaration of Independence and later during the Constitutional Convention. His early career, however, is well described. The following selection from the Autobiography tells of Franklin's arrival in Philadelphia at the age of 17 after running away from home in Boston.

I WAS in my working dress, my best clothes being to come round by sea. I was dirty from my journey; my pockets were stuffed out with shirts and stockings; I knew no soul nor where to look for lodging. I was fatigued with traveling, rowing, and want of rest; I was very hungry; and my whole stock of cash consisted of a Dutch dollar and about a shilling in copper. The latter I gave the people of the boat for my passage, who at first refused it, on account of my rowing; but I insisted on their taking it, a man being sometimes more generous when he has but a little money than when he has plenty, perhaps through fear of being thought to have but little.

Then I walked up the street, gazing about, till near the market-house I met a boy with bread. I had made many a meal on bread, and, inquiring where he got it, I went immediately to the baker's he directed me to, in Second Street, and asked for biscuit, intending such as we had in Boston; but they, it seems, were not made in Philadelphia. Then I asked for a three-penny loaf, and was told they had none such. So, not considering or knowing the difference of money, and the greater cheapness nor the names of his bread, I bade him give me three-penny-worth of any sort. He gave me, accordingly, three great puffy rolls. I was surprised at the quantity, but took it, and, having no room in my pockets, walked off with a roll under each arm, and eating the other. Thus I went up Market Street as far as Fourth Street, passing by the door of Mr. Read, my future wife's father; when she, standing at the door, saw me, and thought I made, as I certainly did, a most awkward, ridiculous appearance. Then I turned and went down Chestnut Street and part of Walnut Street, eating my roll all the way, and, coming round, found myself again at Market Street wharf, near the boat I came in, to which I went for a draught of the river water; and, being filled with one of my rolls, gave the other two to a woman and her child that came down the river in the boat with us, and were waiting to go farther.

Thus refreshed, I walked again up the street, which by this time had many clean-dressed people in it, who were all walking the same way. I joined them, and thereby was led into the great meetinghouse of the Quakers near the market. I sat down among them, and, after looking round awhile and hearing nothing said, being very drowsy through labor and want of rest the preceding night, I fell fast asleep, and continued so till the meeting broke up, when one was kind enough to rouse me. This was, therefore, the first house I was in, or slept in, in Philadelphia.

Walking down again toward the river and looking in the faces of people, I met a young Quaker man, whose countenance I liked and accosting him, requested he would tell me where a stranger could get lodging. We were then near the sign of the Three Mariners. "Here," says he, "is one place that entertains strangers, but it is not a reputable house; if thee wilt walk with me, I'll show thee a better." He brought me to the Crooked Billet in Water Street. Here I got a dinner; and while I was eating it several sly questions were asked me, as it seemed to be suspected from my youth and appearance that I might be some runaway.

After dinner my sleepiness returned, and, being shown to a bed, I lay down without undressing, and slept till six in the evening, was called to supper, went to bed again very early, and slept soundly till next morning. Then I made myself as tidy as I could and went to Andrew Bradford the printer's. I found in the shop the old man his father, whom I had seen at New York, and who, traveling on horseback, had got to Philadelphia before me. He introduced me to his son, who received me civilly, gave me a breakfast, but told me he did not at present want a hand, being lately supplied with one; but there was another printer in town, lately set up, one Keimer, who perhaps might employ me; if not, I should be welcome to lodge at his house, and he would give me a little work to do now and then till fuller business should offer.

The old gentleman said he would go with me to the new printer; and when we found him, "Neighbor," says Bradford, "I have brought to see you a young man of your business; perhaps you may want such a one." He asked me a few questions, put a composing stick in my hand to see how I worked, and then said he would employ me soon, though he had just then nothing for me to do; and, taking old Bradford, whom he · had never seen before, to be of the town's people that had a good will for him, entered into a conversation on his present undertaking and prospects; while Bradford, not discovering that he was the other printer's father, on Keimer's saying he expected soon to get the greatest part of the business into his own hands, drew him on by artful questions, and starting little doubts, to explain all his views, what interest he relied on, and in what manner he intended to proceed. I, who stood by and heard all, saw immediately that one of them was a crafty old sophister, and the other a mere novice. Bradford left me with Keimer, who was greatly surprised when I told him who the old man was.

Keimer's printing-house, I found, consisted of an old shattered press, and one small, worn-out font of English [type], which he was then using himself, composing an elegy on Aquila Rose, before mentioned, an ingenious young man, of excellent character, much respected in the town, clerk of the Assembly, and a pretty poet. Keimer made verses too, but very indifferently. He could not be said to write them, for his manner was to compose them in the types directly out of his head. So there being no copy, but one pair of cases, and the elegy likely to require all the letters, no one could help him. I endeavored to put his press (which he had not yet used, and of which he understood nothing) into order fit to be worked with; and, promising to come and print off his elegy as soon as he should have got it ready, I returned to Bradford's, who gave me a little job to do for the present, and there I lodged and dieted. A few days after, Keimer sent for me to print off the elegy. And now he had got another pair of cases, and a pamphlet to reprint, on which he set me to work.

These two printers I found poorly qualified for their business. Bradford had not been bred to it, and was very illiterate; and Keimer, though something of a scholar, was a mere compositor, knowing nothing of presswork. He had been one of the French prophets [a group of French Protestants known as Camisards, persecuted under Louis XIV], and could act their enthusiastic agitations. At this time he did not profess any particular religion, but something of all on occasion; was very ignorant of the world, and had, as I afterward found, a good deal of the knave in his composition. He did not like my lodging at Bradford's while I worked with him. He had a house, indeed, but without furniture, so he could not lodge me; but he got me a lodging at Mr. Read's, before mentioned, who was the owner of his house; and, my chest and clothes being come by this time, I made rather a more respectable appearance in the eyes of Miss Read than I had done when she first happened to see me eating my roll in the street.

I began now to have some acquaintance among the young people of the town that were lovers of reading, with whom I spent my evenings very pleasantly; and gaining money by my industry and frugality, I lived very agreeably, forgetting Boston as much as I could, and not desiring that any there should know where I resided.

Franklin was an industrious, ambitious young man who had thoroughly mastered the trade of printer before leaving Boston. In Philadelphia, he set up his own printing business and prospered so much that he was able to retire at the age of 42. The rest of his life he devoted to public enterprises and to scientific investigation. He was instrumental in founding a hospital, the academy that became the University of Pennsylvania, and the American Philosophical Society. He initiated projects for providing police protection, street lighting, cleaning, and paving in Philadelphia. He served, as postmaster-general for the colonies, and later represented them in England as events moved toward the Revolution.

> One of his many public-spirited projects was the establishment of a lending library, and in the selection that follows he tells just how he got the library started.

AT the time I established myself in Pennsylvania, there was not a good bookseller's shop in any of the colonies to the southward of Boston. In New York and Philadelphia the printers were indeed stationers; they sold only paper, etc., almanacs, ballads, and a few common school-books. Those who loved reading were obliged to send for their books from England; the members of the Junto [Franklin's club] had each a few. We had left the alehouse, where we first met, and hired a room to hold our club in. I proposed that we should all of us bring our books to that room, where they would not only be ready to consult in our conferences, but become a common benefit, each of us being at liberty to borrow such as he wished to read at home. This was accordingly done, and for some time contented us.

Finding the advantage of this little collection, I proposed to render the benefit from books more common, by commencing a public subscription library. I drew a sketch of the plan and rules that would be necessary, and got a skilful conveyancer, Mr. Charles Brockden, to put the whole in form of articles of agreement to be subscribed, by which each subscriber engaged to pay a certain sum down for the first purchase of books, and an annual contribution for increasing them. So few were the readers at that time in Philadelphia, and the majority of us so poor, that I was not able, with great industry, to find more than fifty persons, mostly young tradesmen, willing to pay down for this purpose forty shillings each, and ten shillings per annum. [A shilling in Franklin's day was worth perhaps $1.50 in today's money.] On this little fund we began. The books were imported; the library was opened one day in the week for lending to the subscribers, on their promissory notes to pay double the value if not duly returned. The institution soon manifested its utility, was imitated by other towns, and in other provinces. The libraries were augmented by donations; reading became fashionable; and our people, having no public amusements to divert their attention from study, became better acquainted with books, and in a few years were observed by strangers to be better instructed and more intelligent than people of the same rank generally are in other countries...

This library afforded me the means of improvement by constant study, for which I set apart an hour or two each day, and thus repaired in some degree the loss of the learned education my father once intended for me. Reading was the only amusement I allowed myself. I spent no time in taverns, games, or frolics of any kind; and my industry in my business continued as indefatigable as it was necessary.

PART TWO

The Times That Tried Men's Souls
1770-1783

Preface

The American Revolution is one of those great events in history whose consequences are still being felt, not alone in our own nation, but in all corners of the globe. It was the first successful overthrow of a monarchy in modern times, and it marked the beginning of an era of world revolutions. America emerged as a new nation and as a republic dedicated to the principles of freedom and equality.

Americans long have debated the causes of the American Revolution. Were the seeds of rebellion actually sown, as Nathaniel Hawthorne suggests in his story "Endicott and the Red Cross," when the Puritans defied the authority of the Church of England? Was the desire for liberty part of the character of the men and women who braved the dangers and suffered the hardships of the New World? Or did the Revolution come about because of England's shortsighted management of her American colonies? Were the economic measures employed by the mother country to restrict American trade and to benefit the merchants and manufacturers of England crucial in bringing on the conflict? These are questions that never can be answered fully.

The truth no doubt lies somewhere in between. The Revolution was fought for independence from an empire which had been unwilling to give America political and economic equality. Those who fought on the patriot side came from all classes and economic groups, and so did the loyalists who fought to uphold the authority of King George III. A good many others took no part in the war, but maintained an uneasy neutrality. The fact that the patriot leaders were in the main upper class and moderate and that the patriot army was commanded by a general who placed the country above his own ambition helps explain why the war was fought to a successful conclusion without a dictatorship or a reign of terror arising, as occurred in the French Revolution later.

One should view the American Revolution not as a modern war in which every citizen is involved—either in military service or in the duties and austerities of the home front—but as a war consisting of a battle here and there, stretched out over a period of seven years and involving thousands rather than millions of people. In addition, one should think of the Revolution as a civil war rather than as a spontaneous uprising of the American colonies to throw off the authority of England. Throughout the colonies, there were many loyalists who actively aided the British. At the same time, in England the colonies had many friends who did not support the British government's conduct of the war.

If causes are hard to establish, the record of events is easy to discern. No one was indifferent to the war, and the descriptions of it and reflections on it are voluminous. We had no trouble getting together a collection of interesting documents to illustrate all phases of the war. Considering the fact that there were no typewriters, no teletype machines, no high-speed rotary presses, no radio or television broadcasting in the eighteenth century, the volume of material written about the war by contemporaries is staggering. An editor's real problem is to decide what to use out of the abundance at his disposal.

The following selections are designed to provide glimpses of the Revolution at crucial points—from the events immediately preceding the outbreak of hostilities to the Peace of Paris in 1783. We have used material illustrating both sides of the military record, that is, garrison life as well as battles, and civilian life in its various political, social, and economic aspects. Yet this booklet can open only a few windows on what Tom Paine called "the times that try men's souls." We hope that these selections will send readers to much larger collections, such as Henry Steele Commager and Richard B. Morris' *The Spirit of 'Seventy-Six,* which contains nearly 1300 pages of primary materials on the Revolution.

In editing the manuscripts in this booklet, we have followed the practice of modernizing punctuation, capitalization, and spelling only when necessary to make the selections clear. We have silently corrected misspelled words and typographical errors. Wherever possible, we have used complete selections, but occasionally space limitations have made necessary cuts in the original documents. Such cuts are indicated by spaced periods. In general, the selections appear as the authors wrote them.

Richard B. Morris
James Woodress

I. The Foreground

THE BOSTON MASSACRE

Five years before the battles of Lexington and Concord, anti-British feeling already was intense in Boston. Opposition to the taxes levied by the Townshend Acts had incited mobs to attack the king's customs officials, and the British government had moved a contingent of soldiers to Boston to maintain order. One day in March, 1770, the event took place that is described below by John Tudor, a Boston merchant who was an eyewitness. This event, the Boston Massacre, is one of the many incidents and circumstances that led eventually to the Declaration of Independence.

ON Monday evening the 5th current, a few minutes after 9 o'clock a most horrid murder· was committed in King Street before the customhouse door by 8 or 9 soldiers under the command of Captain Thomas Preston drawn off from the main guard on the south side of the Townhouse.

This unhappy affair began by some boys and young fellows throwing snowballs at the sentry placed at the customhouse door. On which 8 or 9 soldiers came to his assistance. Soon after a number of people collected, when the Captain commanded the soldiers to fire, which they did, and three men were killed on the spot and several mortally wounded, one of which died the next morning. The Captain soon drew off his soldiers up to the main guard, or the consequences might have been terrible, for on the guns firing the people were alarmed and set the bells a-ringing as if for fire, which drew multitudes to the place of action.

Lt. Governor Hutchinson, who was commander-in-chief, was sent for and came to the Council Chamber, where some of the magistrates attended. The Governor desired the multitude about ten o'clock to separate and go home peaceably and he would do all in his power that justice should be done. The 29th Regiment was then under arms on the south side of the Townhouse, but the people insisted that the soldiers should be ordered to their barracks first before they would separate, which being done the people separated about one o'clock.

Captain Preston was taken up by a warrant given to the high sheriff by Justices Dana and Tudor and came under examination about two o'clock, and we sent him to jail soon after three, having evidence sufficient to commit him, on his ordering the soldiers to fire: so about four o'clock the town became quiet. The next forenoon the eight soldiers that fired on the inhabitants were also sent to jail. Tuesday morning the inhabitants met at Faneuil Hall and after some pertinent speeches, chose a committee of fifteen gentlemen to wait on the Lt. Governor in Council to request the immediate removal of the troops. The message was in these words:

"It is the unanimous opinion of this meeting that the inhabitants and soldiery can no longer live together in safety; that nothing can rationally be expected to restore the peace of the town and prevent blood and carnage but the removal of the troops. We most fervently pray his Honor that his power and influence may be exerted for their instant removal."

His Honor's reply was: "Gentlemen, I am extremely sorry for the unhappy difference and especially of the last evening." He signified that it was not in his power to remove the troops, etc., etc.

The above reply was not satisfactory to the inhabitants, as but one regiment should be removed to the Castle barracks. In the afternoon the town adjourned to Dr. Sewall's meetinghouse, for Faneuil Hall was not large enough to hold the people, there being at least three thousand, some supposed near four thousand, when they chose a committee to wait on the Lt. Governor to let him and the Council know that nothing less would satisfy the people than a total and immediate removal of the troops out of the town.

His Honor laid before the Council the vote of the town. The Council thereon expressed themselves to be unanimously of the opinion that it was absolutely necessary for his majesty's service, the good order of the town, etc. that the troops should be immediately removed out of the town. His Honor communicated this advice of the Council to Col. Dalrymple and desired he would order the troops down to Castle William. After the Colonel had seen the vote of the Council, he gave his word and honor to the town's committee that both the regiments should be removed without delay. The committee returned to the town meeting and Mr. Hancock, chairman of the committee, read their report as above, which was received with a shout and clap of hands, which made the meetinghouse ring: so the meeting was dissolved and a great number of gentlemen appeared to watch the center of the town and the prison, which continued for eleven nights and all was quiet again, as the soldiers were all moved off to the Castle.

Thursday, agreeable to a general request of the inhabitants, were followed to the grave (for they were all buried in one) in succession the four bodies of Messrs. Samuel Gray, Samuel Maverick, James Caldwell and Crisp us Attucks, the unhappy victims who fell in the bloody massacre. On this sorrowful occasion most of the shops and stores in town were shut; all the bells were ordered to toll a solemn peal in Boston, Charleston, Cambridge, and Roxbury.

The several hearses forming a junction in King Street, the theatre of that inhuman tragedy, proceeded from thence through the main street, lengthened by an immense concourse of people, so numerous as to be obliged to follow in ranks of four and six abreast and brought up by a long train of carriages. The sorrow visible in the countenances, together with the peculiar solemnity, surpass description. It was supposed that the spectators and those that followed the corpses amounted to 15,000, some supposed 20,000.

Captain Preston was tried for his life on the affair of the above on October 24, 1770. The trial lasted five days, but the jury brought him in not guilty.

> It is interesting to note that John Adams was the lawyer who defended the British soldiers at the trial. It took courage to do this in the face of hostile public opinion, but Adams felt that the soldiers had acted in self-defense, and he believed passionately in justice.

THE BOSTON TEA PARTY

Another celebrated event which helped push the colonies towards revolution was the Boston Tea Party. Like the Massacre, it too had its origin in economic grievances. When the British government gave the East India Company a monopoly on the sale of tea, Boston merchants protested violently. The public supported the merchants; and upon the arrival of three ships loaded with tea, the people refused to allow the vessels to be unloaded. Then on the night of December 16, 1773, two hundred "Indians" boarded the ships and dumped the tea into the harbor—342 chests of it, worth 18,000 English pounds.

This destruction of property was deplored by conservatives and liberals alike. Even such a colonial leader as Franklin thought the East India Company should be compensated. But the radicals in Boston remained defiant. One of them even composed a song for the occasion.

> RALLY, Mohawks! bring out your axes,
> And tell King George we'll pay no taxes

> On his foreign tea;
> His threats are vain, and vain to think
> To force our girls and wives to drink
> His vile Bohea! [tea]
> Then rally, boys, and hasten on
> To meet our chiefs at the Green Dragon [inn].

The account of the Tea Party which follows is a recollection of the event by one of the participants. He is George Hewes, who was one of the "Indians" on that momentous night.

The tea destroyed was contained in three ships, lying near each other at what was called at that time Griffin's wharf, and were surrounded by armed ships of war. The commanders had publicly declared that if the rebels, as they were pleased to style the Bostonians, should not withdraw their opposition to the landing of the tea before a certain day, the 17th day of December, 1773, they should on that day force it on shore, painted as I was, and who fell in with me and marched in order to the place of our destination.

When we arrived at the wharf, there were three of our number who assumed an authority to direct our operations, to which we readily submitted. They divided us into three parties, for the purpose of boarding the three ships which contained the tea at the same time. The name of him who commanded the division to which I was assigned was Leonard Pitt. The names of the other commanders I never knew. We were immediately ordered by the respective commanders to board all the ships at the same time, which we promptly obeyed.

The commander of the division to which I belonged, as soon as we were on board the ship, appointed me boatswain, and ordered me to go to the captain and demand of him the keys to the hatches and a dozen candles. I made the demand accordingly, and the captain promptly replied, and delivered the articles; but requested me at the same time to do no damage to the ship or rigging. We then were ordered by our commander to open the hatches and take out all the chests of tea and throw them overboard, and we immediately proceeded to execute his orders, first cutting and splitting the chests with our tomahawks, so as thoroughly to expose them to the effects of the water.

In about three hours from the time we went on board, we had thus broken and thrown overboard every tea chest to be found in the ship, while those in the other ships were disposing of the tea in the same way, at the same time. We were surrounded by British armed ships, but no attempt was made to resist us.

We then quietly retired to our several places of residence, without having any conversation with each other, or taking any measures to discover who were our associates; nor do I recollect of our having had the knowledge of the name of a single individual concerned in that affair, except that of Leonard Pitt, the commander of my division, whom I have mentioned. There appeared to be an understanding that each individual should volunteer his services, keep his own secret, and risk the consequence for himself. No disorder took place during that transaction, and it was observed at that time that the stillest night ensued that Boston had enjoyed for many months. under the cover of their cannon's mouth. On the day preceding the seventeenth, there was a meeting of the citizens of the county of Suffolk, convened at one of the churches in Boston, for the purpose of consulting on what measures might be considered expedient to prevent the landing of the tea, or secure the people from the collection of the duty. At that meeting a committee was appointed to wait on Governor Hutchinson, and request him to inform them whether he would take any measures to satisfy the people on the object of the meeting.

To the first application of this committee, the Governor told them he would give them a definite answer by five o'clock in the afternoon. At the hour appointed, the committee again repaired to the Governor's house, and on inquiry found he had gone to his country seat at Milton, a distance of about six miles. When the committee returned and informed the meeting of the absence of the Governor, there was a confused murmur among the members, and the meeting was immediately dissolved, many of them crying out, "Let every man do his duty, and be true to his country"; and there was a general huzza for Griffin's wharf.

It was now evening, and I immediately dressed myself in the costume of an Indian, equipped with a small hatchet, which I and my associates denominated the tomahawk, and a club. After having painted my face and hands with coal dust in the shop of a blacksmith, I repaired to Griffin's wharf, where the ships lay that contained the tea. When I first appeared in the street after being thus disguised, I fell in with many who were dressed, equipped and painted as I was, and who fell in with me and marched in order to the place of our destination.

When we arrived at the wharf, there were three of our number who assumed an authority to direct our operations, to which we readily submitted. They divided us into three parties, for the purpose of boarding the three ships which contained the tea at the same time. The name of him who commanded the division to which I was assigned was Leonard Pitt. The names of the other commanders I never knew. We were immediately ordered by the respective commanders to board all the ships at the same time, which we promptly obeyed.

The commander of the division to which I belonged, as soon as we were on board the ship, appointed me boatswain, and ordered me to go to the captain and demand of him the keys to the hatches and a dozen candles. I made the demand accordingly, and the captain promptly replied, and delivered the articles; but requested me at the same time to do no damage to the ship or rigging. We then were ordered by our commander to open the hatches and take out all the chests of tea and throw them overboard, and we immediately proceeded to execute his orders, first cutting and splitting the chests with our tomahawks, so as thoroughly to expose them to the effects of the water.

In about three hours from the time we went on board, we had thus broken and thrown overboard every tea chest to be found in the ship, while those in the other ships were disposing of the tea in the same way, at the same time. We were surrounded by British armed ships, but no attempt was made to resist us.

We then quietly retired to our several places of residence, without having any conversation with each other, or taking any measures to discover who were our associates; nor do I recollect of our having had the knowledge of the name of a single individual concerned in that affair, except that of Leonard Pitt, the commander of my division, whom I have mentioned. There appeared to be an understanding that each individual should volunteer his services, keep his own secret, and risk the consequence for himself. No disorder took place during that transaction, and it was observed at that time that the stillest night ensued that Boston had enjoyed for many months.

During the time we were throwing the tea overboard, there were several attempts made by some of the citizens of Boston and its vicinity to carry off small quantities of it for their family use. To effect that object, they would watch their opportunity to snatch up a handful from the deck, where it became plentifully scattered, and put it into their pockets. One Captain O'Connor, whom I well knew, came on board for that purpose, and when he supposed he was not noticed, filled his pockets, and also the lining of his coat. But I had detected him and gave information to the captain of what he was doing. We were ordered to take him into custody, and just as he was stepping from the vessel, I seized him by the skirt of his coat, and in attempting to pull him back, I tore it off; but, springing forward, by a rapid effort he made his escape. He had, however, to run a gauntlet through the crowd upon the wharf, each one, as he passed, giving him a kick or a stroke.

Another attempt was made to save a little tea from the ruins of the cargo by a tall, aged man who wore a large cocked hat and white wig, which was fashionable at that time. He had sleightly [secretly] slipped a little into his pocket, but being detected, they seized him and, taking his hat and wig from his head, threw them, together with the tea, of which they had emptied his pockets, into the water. In consideration of his advanced age, he was permitted to escape, with now and then a slight kick.

The next morning, after we had cleared the ships of the tea, it was discovered that very considerable quantities of it were floating upon the surface of the water; and to prevent the possibility of any of its being saved for use, a number of small boats were manned by sailors and citizens, who rowed them into those parts of the harbor wherever the tea was visible, and by beating it with oars and paddles so thoroughly drenched it as to render its entire destruction inevitable.

Governor Hutchinson, the king's chief officer in Massachusetts, was powerless to enforce unpopular laws, though he did his best to thwart the mob. When the fiery Sam Adams called a mass meeting to support the radicals, the governor made strenuous objections. Hutchinson from the Tea Party. Several years later he wrote an account of the affair, from which we quote two paragraphs:

THE governor, seeing the powers of government thus taken out of the hands of the legally established authority, could not justify a total silence, though he knew he could say nothing which would check the usurpers. He sent the sheriff with a proclamation to be read in the meeting, bearing testimony against it as an unlawful assembly, and requiring the moderator and the people present forthwith to separate at their peril. The sheriff desired leave to read the directions he had received from the governor, which was granted; but the reading of the proclamation was opposed, until Mr. Adams signified his acquiescence. Being read, a general hiss followed, and then a question whether they would surcease all further proceedings, saw perhaps more clearly than most people the consequences that were to follow as the governor required, which was determined in the negative....

This was the boldest stroke which had yet been struck in America. The people in all parts of the province showed more or less concern at the expected consequences. They were, however, at a distance; something might intervene to divert them. Besides, the thing was done: there was no way of nullifying it. Their leaders feared no consequences. To engage the people in some desperate measure had long been their plan. They never discovered more concern than when the people were quiet upon the repeal of an act of Parliament, or upon concessions made or assurances given; and never more satisfaction than when government had taken any new measures, or appeared to be inclined to them, tending, or which might be improved, to irritate and disturb the people. They had nothing to fear for themselves. They had gone too far to recede. If the colonies were subject to the supreme authority and laws of Great Britain, their offenses, long since, had been of the highest nature. Their all depended upon attaining to the object which first engaged them. There was no way of attaining to it but by involving the body of the people in the same circumstances they were in themselves. And it is certain that ever after this time an opinion was easily instilled, and was continually increasing, that the body of the people had also gone too far to recede, and that an open and general revolt must be the consequence; and it was not long before actual preparations were visibly making for it in most parts of the province.

PAUL REVERE'S RIDE

"Listen, my children, and you shall hear
Of the midnight ride of Paul Revere."

Thus begins Longfellow's well-known poem describing the part Paul Revere played in alerting the Massachusetts farmers on the night before the first battle of the Revolution. The poet took some liberties with the facts, as you will see in the following account written by Paul Revere himself. Revere never reached Concord but was captured by the British between Lexington and his destination. Fact and fiction agree, however, that he did sound the alarm during that famous night.

The events leading up to Paul Revere's ride may be summarized easily. The British commander in Boston, General Gage, planned to seize military supplies stored by the Americans in Concord. The patriots found out about the plans and sent two messengers, one of whom was Paul Revere, to Lexington and Concord. The next day there occurred the fighting between the minutemen and British that included what Ralph Waldo Emerson later called "the shot heard round the world."

Here is Paul Revere remembering the night of April 18, 1775, in a letter to Dr. Jeremy Belknap written twenty-three years later:

In the fall of 1774 and winter of 1775, I was one of upwards of thirty, chiefly mechanics, who formed ourselves into a committee for the purpose of watching the movements of the British soldiers, and gaining every intelligence of the movements of the Tories. We held our meetings at the Green Dragon tavern. We were so careful that our meetings should be kept secret that every time we met, every person swore upon the Bible that they would not discover any of our transactions but to Messrs. Hancock, Adams, Doctors Warren, Church and one or two more....

In the winter, towards the spring, we frequently took turns, two and two, to watch the soldiers by patrolling the streets all night. The Saturday night preceding the 19th of April, about 12 o'clock at night, the boats belonging to the transports were all launched and carried under the sterns of the men-of-war. (They had been previously hauled up and repaired.) We likewise found that the grenadiers and light infantry were all taken off duty.

From these movements we expected something serious was to be transacted. On Tuesday evening, the 18th, it was observed that a number of soldiers were marching towards the bottom of the Common. About 10 o'clock, Dr. Warren sent in great haste for me and begged that I would immediately set off for Lexington, where Messrs. Hancock and Adams were, and acquaint them of the movement, and that it was thought they were the objects.

When I got to Dr. Warren's house, I found he had sent an express by land to Lexington—a Mr. William Daws. The Sunday before, by desire of Dr. Warren, I had been to Lexington, to Messrs. Hancock and Adams, who were at the Rev. Mr. Clark's. I [had] returned at night through Charlestown; there I [had] agreed with a Colonel Conant and some other gentlemen that if the British went out by water, we would show two lanthorns in the North Church steeple; and if by land, one, as a signal; for we were apprehensive it would be difficult to cross the Charles River or get over Boston Neck. I left Dr. Warren, called upon a friend and desired him to make the signals.

I then went home, took my boots and surtout [overcoat], went to the north part of the town, where I had kept a boat; two friends rowed me across Charles River, a little to the eastward where the Somerset man-of-war lay. It was then young flood, the ship was winding, and the moon was rising. They landed me on the Charlestown side. When I got into town, I met Colonel Conant and several others; they said they had seen our signals. I told them what was acting, and went to get me a horse; I got a horse of Deacon Larkin. While the horse was preparing, Richard Devens, Esq., who was one of the Committee of Safety, came to me and told me that he came down the road from Lexington after sundown that evening; that he met ten British officers, all well mounted, and armed, going up the road.

I set off upon a very good horse; it was then about eleven o'clock and very pleasant. After I had passed Charlestown Neck...I saw two men on horseback under a tree. When I got near them, I discovered they were British officers. One tried to get ahead of me, and the other to take me. I turned my horse very quick and galloped towards Charlestown Neck, and then pushed for the Medford Road. The one who chased me, endeavoring to cut me off, got into a clay pond near where Mr. Russell's Tavern is now built. I got clear of him, and went through Medford, over the bridge and up to Menotomy. In Medford, I awaked the captain of the minute men; and after that, I alarmed almost every house, till I got to Lexington. I found Messrs. Hancock and Adams at the Rev. Mr. Clark's; I told them my errand and inquired for Mr. Daws; they said he had not been there; I related the story of the two officers, and supposed that he must have been stopped, as he ought to have been there before me.

After I had been there about half an hour, Mr. Daws came; we refreshed ourselves, and set off for Concord. We were overtaken by a young Dr. Prescott, whom we found to be a high Son of Liberty. I told them of the ten officers that Mr. Devens met, and that it was probable we might be stopped before we got to Concord; for I supposed that after night they divided themselves, and that two of them had fixed themselves in such passages as were most likely to stop any intelligence going to Concord. I likewise mentioned that we had better alarm all the inhabitants till we got to Concord. The young doctor much approved of it and said he would stop with either of us, for the people between that and Concord knew him and would give the more credit to what we said.

We had got nearly half way. Mr. Daws and the doctor stopped to alarm the people of a house. I was about one hundred rods ahead when I saw two men in nearly the same situation as those officers were near Charlestown. I called for the doctor and Mr. Daws to come up. In an instant I was surrounded by four. They had placed themselves in a straight road that inclined each way; they had taken down a pair of bars on the north side of the road, and two of them were under a tree in the pasture. The doctor being foremost, he came up and we tried to get past them; but they being armed with pistols and swords, they forced us into the pasture. The doctor jumped his horse over a low stone wall and got to Concord.

I observed a wood at a small distance and made for that. When I got there, out started six officers on horseback and ordered me to dismount. One of them, who appeared to have the command, examined me, where I came from and what my name was. I told him. He asked me if I was an express. I answered in the affirmative. He demanded what time I left Boston. I told him, and added that their troops had catched aground· in passing the river, and that there would be five hundred Americans there in a short time, for I had alarmed the country all the way up. He immediately rode towards those who stopped us, when all five of them came down upon a full gallop. One of them, whom I afterwards found to be a Major Mitchel, of the 5th Regiment, clapped his pistol to my head, called me by name and told me he was going to ask me some questions, and if I did not give him true answers, he would blow my brains out. He then asked me similar questions to those above. He then ordered me to mount my horse, after searching me for arms. He then ordered them to advance and to lead me in front. When we got to the road, they turned down towards Lexington. When we had got about one mile, the major rode up to the officer that was leading me, and told him to give me to the sergeant. As soon as he took me, the major ordered him, if I attempted to run, or anybody insulted them, to blow my brains out.

We rode till we got near Lexington meeting-house, when the militia fired a volley of guns, which appeared to alarm them very much. The major inquired of me how far it was to Cambridge, and if there were any other road. After some consultation, the major rode up to the sergeant and asked if his horse was tired. He answered him he was—he was a sergeant of grenadiers and had a small horse. "Then," said he, "take that man's horse." I dismounted, and the sergeant mounted my horse, when they all rode towards Lexington meeting-house.

I went across the burying-ground and some pastures and came to the Rev. Mr. Clark's house, where I found Messrs. Hancock and Adams. I told them of my treatment, and they concluded to go from that house towards Woburn. I went with them and a Mr. Lowell, who was a clerk to Mr. Hancock.

When we got to the house where they intended to stop, Mr. Lowell and myself returned to Mr. Clark's, to find what was going on. When we got there, an elderly man came in; he said he had just come from the tavern, that a man had come from Boston who said there were no British troops coming. Mr. Lowell and myself went towards the tavern, when we met a man on a full gallop, who told us the troops were coming up the rocks. We afterwards met another, who said they were close by. Mr. Lowell asked me to go to the tavern with him, to get a trunk of papers belonging to Mr. Hancock. We went up chamber [upstairs], and while we were getting the trunk, we saw the British very near, upon a full march. We hurried towards Mr. Clark's house. In our way we passed through the militia. There were about fifty. When we had got about one hundred yards from the meeting-house, the British troops appeared on both sides of the meeting-house. In their front was an officer on horseback. They made a short halt; when I saw, and heard, a gun fired, which appeared to be a pistol. Then I could distinguish two guns, and then a continual roar of musketry; when we made off with the trunk.

THE BATTLE OF LEXINGTON

While Paul Revere was helping carry the trunk away from the tavern, the Revolution was beginning on the village green across the road. There are many accounts of the Battle of Lexington, and many of the details contradict each other. The historian cannot be sure just who fired the first shot. In the following pages we have printed accounts of the battle from both sides. The first was written on the day of the engagement by a British soldier, who was much more impressed by the fighting at Concord and the retreat. He sums up the minor skirmish at Lexington in one paragraph. The second account was written a year later by the Reverend Jonas Clark, who had been an eyewitness, though not a participant in the battle.

Here is the report of the British officer, presumably Lt. John Barker of the King's Own Regiment:

1775, April 19th. LAST night between 10 and 11 o'clock all the Grenadiers and Light Infantry of the army, making about 600 men (under the command of Lt. Col. Smith of the 10th and Major Pitcairn of the Marines), embarked and were landed upon the opposite shore on Cambridge Marsh; few but the commanding officers knew what expedition we were going upon. After getting over the marsh, where we were wet up to the knees, we were halted in a dirty road and stood there till two o'clock in the morning, waiting for provisions to be brought from the boats and to be divided, and which most of the men threw away, having carried some with 'em. At 2 o'clock we began our march by wading through a very long ford up to our middles. After going· a few miles we took 3 or 4 people who were going off to give intelligence.

About 5 miles on this side of a town called Lexington, which lay in our road, we heard there were some hundreds of people collected together intending to oppose us and stop our going on. At 5 o'clock we arrived there and saw a number of people, I believe between 2 and 300, formed in a common in the middle of the town. We still continued advancing, keeping prepared against l).n attack tho' without intending to attack them; but on our coming near them they fired one or two shots, upon which our men without any orders rushed in upon them, fired and put 'em to flight. Several of them were killed; we could not tell how many because they were got behind walls and into the woods. We had a man of the 10th Light Infantry wounded, nobody else hurt. We then formed on the common, but with some difficulty, the men were so wild they could hear no orders.

> Here is the account of Jonas Clark, who was pastor of the church in Lexington:

BETWEEN 3 and 4 o'clock, one of the expresses returned, informing that there was no appearance of the troops on the roads either from Cambridge or Charlestown; and that it was supposed that the movements in the army the evening before were only a feint to alarm the people. Upon this, therefore, the militia company were dismissed for the present, but with orders to be within call of the drum—waiting the return of the other messenger, who was expected in about an hour, or sooner, if any discovery should be made of the motions of the troops. But he was prevented by their silent and sudden arrival at the place where he was waiting for intelligence. So that, after all this precaution, we had no notice of their approach till the brigade was actually in the town and upon a quick march within about a mile and a quarter of the meeting house and place of parade.

However, the commanding officer thought best to call the company together, not with any design of opposing so superior a force, much less of commencing hostilities, but only with a view to determine what to do, when and where to meet, and to dismiss and disperse.

Accordingly, about half an hour after four o'clock, alarm guns were fired, and the drums beat to arms, and the militia were collecting together. Some, to the number of about 50 or 60, or possibly more, were on the parade, others were coming towards it. In the mean time, the troops having thus stolen a march upon us and, to prevent any intelligence of their approach, having seized and held prisoners several persons whom they met unarmed upon the road, seemed to come determined for murder and bloodshed—and that whether provoked to it or not! When within about half a quarter of a mile of the meeting-house, they halted, and the command was given to prime and load; which being done, they marched on till they came up to the east end of said meeting-house, in sight of our militia (collecting as aforesaid) who were about 12 or 13 rods distant.

Immediately upon their appearing so suddenly and so nigh, Capt. Parker, who commanded the militia company, ordered the men to disperse and take care of themselves, and not to fire. Upon this, our men dispersed—but many of them not so speedily as they might have done, not having the most distant idea of such brutal barbarity and more than savage cruelty from the troops of a British king, as they immediately experienced! For, no sooner did they come in sight of our company, but one of them, supposed to be an officer of rank, was heard to say to the troops, "Damn them! We will have them!" Upon which the troops shouted aloud, huzza'd, and rushed furiously towards our men.

About the same time, three officers (supposed to be Col. Smith, Major Pitcairn, and another officer) advanced on horse back to the front of the body, and coming within 5 or 6 rods of the militia, one of them cried out, "Ye villains, ye Rebels, disperse! Damn you, disperse!"—or words to this effect! One of them (whether the same or not is not easily determined) said, "Lay down your arms! Damn you, why don't you lay down your arms?" The second of these officers, about this time, fired a pistol towards the militia as they were dispersing. The foremost, who was within a few yards of our men, brandishing his sword and then pointing towards them, with a loud voice said to the troops, "Fire! By God, fire!"—which was instantly followed by a discharge of arms from the said troops, succeeded by a very heavy and close fire upon our party, dispersing, so long as any of them were within reach. Eight were left dead upon the ground! Ten were wounded. The rest of the company, through divine goodness, were (to a miracle) preserved unhurt in this murderous action! . . .

One circumstance more before the brigade quitted Lexington, I beg leave to mention, as what may give a further specimen of the spirit and character of the officers and men of this body of troops. After the militia company were dispersed and the firing ceased, the troops drew up and formed in a body on the common, fired a volley and gave three huzzas, by way of triumph and as expressive of the joy of victory and glory of conquest! Of this transaction, I was a witness, having, at that time, a fair view of their motions and being at the distance of not more than 70 or 80 rods from them.

THE BATTLE OF CONCORD

After the brief skirmish at Lexington, the British continued on to Concord to carry out their mission of destroying supplies. What happened there is vividly described in the diary of William Emerson (grandfather of Ralph Waldo Emerson), whose house stood beside the Concord River and near the bridge where the battle took place.

1775, 19 April. THIS morning, between 1 and 2 o'clock, we were alarmed by the ringing of the bell, and upon examination found that the troops, to the number of 800, had stole their march from Boston, in boats and barges, from the bottom of the Common over to a point in Cambridge, near to Inman's farm, and were at Lexington Meetinghouse, half an hour before sunrise, where they had fired upon a body of our men, and (as we afterward heard) had killed several.

This intelligence was brought us at first by Dr. Samuel Prescott [Paul Revere's companion], who narrowly escaped the guard that were sent before on horses, purposely to prevent all posts and messengers from giving us timely information. He, by the help of a very fleet horse, crossing several walls and fences, arrived at Concord at the time above mentioned; when several posts were immediately dispatched, that returning confirmed the account of the regulars' arrival at Lexington, and that they were on their way to Concord.

Upon this, a number of our minute men belonging to this town, and Acton and Lincoln, with several others that were in readiness, marched out to meet them, while the alarm company were preparing to receive them in the town. Capt. Minot, who commanded them, thought it proper to take possession of the hill above the meeting-house, as the most advantageous situation. No sooner had our men gained it than we were met by the companies that were sent out to meet the troops, who informed us that they were just upon us, and that we must retreat, as their number was more than treble ours.

We then retreated from the hill near the Liberty Pole and took a new post back of the town upon an eminence, where we formed into two battalions and waited the arrival of the enemy. Scarcely had we formed before we saw the British troops at the distance of a quarter of a mile, glittering in arms, advancing towards us with the greatest celerity. Some were for making a stand, notwithstanding the superiority of their number; but others more prudent thought best to retreat till our strength should be equal to the enemy's by recruits from neighboring towns that were continually coming to our assistance.

Accordingly we retreated over the bridge, when the troops came into the town, set fire to several carriages for the artillery, destroyed 60 barrels [of] flour, rifled several houses, took possession of the town-house, destroyed 500 lb. of balls, set a guard of 100 men at the North Bridge, and sent up a party to the house of Col. Barrett, where they were in expectation of finding a quantity of warlike stores. But these were happily secured just before their arrival, by transportation into the woods and other by-places.

In the meantime, the guard set by the enemy to secure the pass at the North Bridge were alarmed by the approach of our people, who had retreated, as mentioned before, and were now advancing with special orders not to fire upon the troops unless fired upon. These orders were so punctually observed that we received the fire of the enemy in three several and separate discharges of their pieces before it was returned by our commanding officer; the firing then soon became general for several minutes, in which skirmish two were killed on each side, and several of the enemy wounded.

It may here be observed, by the way, that we were the more cautious to prevent beginning a rupture with the King's troops, as we were then uncertain what had happened at Lexington, and knew [not] that they had begun the quarrel there by first firing upon our people and killing eight men upon the spot.

The three companies of troops soon quitted their post at the bridge and retreated in the greatest disorder and confusion to the main body, who were soon upon the march to meet them; For half an hour, the enemy, by their marches and countermarches, discovered great fickleness and inconstancy of mind, sometimes advancing, sometimes returning to their former posts; till at length they quitted the town and retreated by the way they came. In the meantime, a party of our men (150) took the back way through the Great Fields into the east quarter and had placed themselves to advantage, lying in ambush behind walls, fences and buildings, ready to fire upon the enemy on their retreat.

THE CAPTURE OF TICONDEROGA

The Continental Congress in Philadelphia had authorized the colonists to defend themselves against the British, but it was not yet ready to approve of offensive action. New Englanders were not content, however, to resist only, as they had done at Lexington and Concord. Both Benedict Arnold and Ethan Allen set out to capture Fort Ticonderoga on Lake Champlain, and on the morning of Moy 10, 1775, the British garrison at Ticonderoga surrendered without firing a shot. This remarkable event yielded the colonists more than 100 cannon and important military stores. The following narrative is Ethan Allen's account of the capture.

EVER since I arrived to a state of manhood and acquainted myself with the general history of mankind, I have felt a sincere passion for liberty. The history of nations doomed to perpetual slavery, in consequence of yielding up to tyrants their natural born liberties, I read with a sort of philosophical horror; so that the first systematical and bloody attempt at Lexington to enslave America thoroughly electrified my mind and fully determined me to take part with my country.

And while I was wishing for an opportunity to signalize myself in its behalf, directions were privately sent to me from the then colony (now state) of Connecticut to raise the Green Mountain Boys, and (if possible) with them to surprise and take the fortress Ticonderoga. This enterprise I cheerfully undertook; and, after first guarding all the several passes that led thither, to cut off all intelligence between the garrison and the country, made a forced march from Bennington and arrived at the lake opposite to Ticonderoga on the evening of the ninth day of May, 1775, with two hundred and thirty valiant Green Mountain Boys; and it was with the utmost difficulty that I procured boats to cross the lake. However, I landed eighty-three men near the garrison, and sent the boats back for the rear guard commanded by Col. Seth Warner. But the day began to dawn, and I found myself under a necessity to attack the fort before the rear could cross the lake; and, as it was viewed hazardous, I harangued the officers and soldiers in the manner following:

"Friends and fellow soldiers, you have, for a number of years past, been a scourge and terror to arbitrary power. Your valour has been famed abroad and acknowledged, as appears by the advice and orders to me (from the general assembly of Connecticut) to surprise and take the garrison now before us. I now propose to advance before you and in person conduct you through the wicketgate; for we must this morning either quit our pretensions to valour, or possess ourselves of this fortress in a few minutes; and, in as much as it is a desperate attempt (which none but the bravest of men dare undertake), I do not urge it on any contrary to his will. You that will undertake voluntarily, poise your firelocks!"

The men being (at this time) drawn up in three ranks, each poised his firelock. I ordered them to face to the right, and, at the head of the centre file, marched them immediately to the wicketgate aforesaid, where I found a sentry posted, who instantly snapped his fusee [flintlock rifle] at me. I ran immediately toward him, and he retreated through the covered way into the parade within the garrison, gave a halloo and ran under a bomb-proof. My party who followed me into the fort, I formed on the parade in such a manner as to face the two barracks which faced each other.

The garrison being asleep (except the sentries), we gave three huzzas which greatly surprised them. One of the sentries made a pass at one of my officers with a charged bayonet and slightly wounded him. My first thought was to kill him with my sword; but, in an instant, altered the design and fury of the blow to a slight cut on the side of the head; upon which he dropped his gun and asked quarter, which I readily granted him, and demanded of him the place where the commanding officer kept. He showed me a pair· of stairs in the front of a barrack, on the west part of the garrison, which led up to a second story in said barrack, to which I immediately repaired, and ordered the commander (Capt. Delaplace) to come forth instantly, or I would sacrifice the whole garrison; at which the captain came immediately to the door with his breeches in his hand. When I ordered him to deliver to me the fort instantly, he asked me by what authority I demanded it; I answered, "In the name of the great Jehovah and the Continental Congress."

The authority of the Congress being very little known at that time, he began to speak again, but I interrupted him and, with my drawn sword over his head, again demanded an immediate surrender of the garrison; to which he then complied, and ordered his men to be forthwith paraded without arms, as he had given up the garrison. In the mean time some of my officers had given orders, and in consequence thereof, sundry of the barrack doors were beat down, and about one third of the garrison imprisoned, which consisted of the said commander, a Lieut. Feltham, a conductor of artillery, a gunner, two sergeants and forty-four rank and file; about one hundred pieces of cannon, one 13-inch mortar and a number of swivels.

This surprise was carried into execution in the gray of the morning of the 10th day of May, 1775. The sun seemed to rise that morning with a superior lustre; and Ticonderoga and its dependencies smiled on its conquerors, who tossed about the flowing bowl and wished success to Congress and the liberty and freedom of America....Col. Warner with the rear guard crossed the lake and joined me early in the morning, whom I sent off without loss of time, with about one hundred men, to take possession of Crown Point, which was garrisoned with a sergeant and twelve men; which he took possession of the same day, as also upwards of one hundred pieces of cannon.

But one thing now remained to be done to make ourselves complete masters of Lake Champlain: this was to possess ourselves of a sloop of war, which was then laying at St. John's; to effect which it was agreed in a council of war to arm and man out a certain schooner, which lay at South Bay, and that Capt. (now General) Arnold should command her, and that I should command the bateaux [small boats]. The necessary preparations being made, we set sail from Ticonderoga in quest of the sloop, which was much larger and carried more guns and heavier metal than the schooner.

General Arnold, with the schooner sailing faster than the bateaux, arrived at St. John's and by surprise possessed himself of the sloop before I could arrive with the bateaux. He also made prisoners of a sergeant and twelve men, who were garrisoned at that place. It is worthy [of] remark that as soon as General Arnold had secured the prisoners on board and had made preparation for sailing, the wind which but a few hours before was fresh in the south and well served to carry us to St. John's, now shifted and came fresh from the north; and in about one hour's time General Arnold sailed with the prize and schooner for Ticonderoga. When I met him with my party, within a few miles of St. John's, he saluted me with a discharge of cannon, which I returned with a volley of small arms. This being repeated three times, I went on board the sloop with my party, where several loyal Congress healths were drank.

We were now masters of Lake Champlain and the garrisons depending thereon.

> Fort Ticonderoga did not remain in American hands. Later in the same year General Arnold, joined by General Richard Montgomery, tried to capture all of Canada. They hoped that French Canadians would join the American colonies and that British troops could be thrown out of the entire northern sector of North America. This, however, was too ambitious an undertaking, and though Montgomery captured Montreal, he and Arnold were beaten disastrously at Quebec. The Americans had to retreat. They remained on the defensive until Arnold, as General Gates' most brilliant subordinate, defeated Burgoyne at Saratoga in 1777.

II. Behind the Lines

DEFIANT WORDS

Although the Revolution properly begins with the battles of Lexington and Concord, more than fourteen months passed before the Declaration of Independence was signed on July 4, 1776. During this time, many sincere people hoped that a complete break with England could be avoided. One of the important events that helped swing public opinion behind the Revolution occurred on January 10, 1776, when a slim pamphlet of 47 pages appeared in Philadelphia. This was Thomas Paine's *Common Sense*, which in a year probably sold 150,000 copies. By the time of the Declaration of Independence, nearly every literate American had read the pamphlet. You can see from the following passages that Paine's words ore very persuasive. The paragraphs we have selected are all from the section of *Common Sense* called "Thoughts on the Present State of American Affairs," though they are not consecutive paragraphs.

In the following pages I offer nothing more than simple facts, plain arguments, and common sense; and have no other preliminaries to settle with the reader, than that he will divest himself of prejudice and prepossession, and suffer his reason and his feeling to determine for themselves; that he will put on, or rather that he will not put off, the true character of a man, and generously enlarge his views beyond the present day.

Volumes have been written on the subject of the struggle between England and America. Men of all ranks have embarked in the controversy, from different motives, and with various designs; but all have been ineffectual, and the period of debate is closed. Arms as the last resource decide the contest; the appeal was the choice of the king, and the continent has accepted the challenge.

The sun never shined on a cause of greater worth. 'Tis not the affair of a city, a county, a province, or a kingdom; but of a continent—of at least one eighth part of the habitable globe. 'Tis not the concern of a day, a year, or an age; posterity are virtually involved in the contest, and will be more or less affected even to the end of time, by the proceedings now. Now is the seed-time of continental union, faith and honor. The least fracture now will be like a name engraved with the point of a pin on the tender rind of a young oak; the wound would enlarge with the tree, and posterity read it in full grown characters.

I have heard it asserted by some, that as America has flourished under her former connection with Great Britain, the same connection is necessary towards her future happiness, and will always have the same effect. Nothing can be more fallacious than this kind of argument. We may as well assert that because a child has thrived upon milk, that it is never to have meat, or that the first twenty years of our lives is to become a precedent for the next twenty. But even this is admitting more than is true; for I answer roundly, that America would have flourished as much, and probably much more, had no European power taken any notice of her. The commerce by which she hath enriched herself are the necessaries of life, and will always have a market while eating is the custom of Europe.

But she has protected us, say some. That she hath engrossed us is true, and defended the continent at our expense as well as her own, is admitted; and she would have defended Turkey from the same motive, *viz.* for the sake of trade and dominion.

But Britain is the parent country, say some. Then the more shame upon her conduct. Even brutes do not devour their young, nor savages make war upon their families; wherefore, the assertion, if true, turns to her reproach; but it happens not to be true....Europe, and not England, is the parent country of America. This new world hath been the asylum for the persecuted lovers of civil and religious liberty from *every part* of Europe. Hither have they fled, not from the tender embraces of the mother, but from the cruelty of the monster; and it is so far true of England, that the same tyranny which drove the first emigrants from home pursues their descendants still.

But, admitting that we were all of English descent, what does it amount to? Nothing. Britain, being now an open enemy, extinguishes every other name and title: and to say that reconciliation is our duty, is truly farcical. The first king of England, of the present line (William the Conqueror) was a Frenchman, and half the peers of England are descendants from the same country; wherefore, by the same method of reasoning, England ought to be governed by France.

Europe is too thickly planted with kingdoms to be long at peace, and whenever a war breaks out between England and any foreign power, the trade of America goes to ruin, *because of her connection with Britain*. The next war may not turn out like the last, and should it not, the advocates for reconciliation now will be wishing for separation then, because neutrality in that case would be a safer convoy than a man of war. Every thing that is right or reasonable pleads for separation. The blood of the slain, the weeping voice of nature cries, 'TIS TIME TO PART. Even the distance at which the Almighty hath placed England and America is a strong and natural proof that the authority of the one over the other, was never the design of heaven. The time likewise at which the continent was discovered, adds weight to the argument, and the manner in which it was peopled, increases the force of it. The Reformation was preceded by the discovery of America: As if the Almighty graciously meant to open a sanctuary to the persecuted in future years, when home should afford neither friendship nor safety.

The authority of Great Britain over this continent, is a form of government, which sooner or later must have an end.

The Declaration of Independence

Words can have a powerful effect in motivating men's actions, and Paine's pamphlet illustrates this truth. Towards the end of Common Sense, Paine called for a Declaration of Independence. Less than six months later Thomas Jefferson, John Adams, and the other framers of the Declaration put their signatures on that historic document. Paine's pamphlet, of course, was not the only thing that accomplished the final break with England, but it was one of the important factors. With the signing of the Declaration, which is too well known to need reprinting here, the war was on in earnest. The signers were well aware that there was no turning back when they wrote:

"WE, THEREFORE, the Representatives of the UNITED STATES OF AMERICA, in General Congress Assembled, appealing to the Supreme Judge of the world for the rectitude of our intentions, do, in the Name and by Authority of the good People of these Colonies, solemnly publish and declare, That these United Colonies are, and of Right ought to be FREE AND INDEPENDENT STATES."

John Adams, who became our second President, was a sober, sensible, hard-working lawyer and nothing like his colleague, the radical Sam Adams. Thus the deep emotion expressed in the following letters that John Adams wrote his wife is all the more remarkable coming, as it does, from a man not given to extravagant language. On July 2, 1776, the Continental Congress passed its resolution of independence, and on the following day Adams wrote his wife Abigail about the event. The day after he wrote the letters, July 4, 1776, Congress approved the Declaration of Independence that Thomas Jefferson and his committee (including John Adams) had written.

JOHN ADAMS TO ABIGAIL ADAMS:

Philadelphia, 3 July, 1776

YESTERDAY the greatest question was decided which ever was debated in America, and a greater, perhaps, never was nor will be decided among men. A resolution was passed without one dissenting colony, "that these United Colonies are, and of right ought to be, free and independent States, and as such they have, and of right ought to have, full power to make war, conclude peace, establish commerce, and to do all other acts and things which other States may rightfully do." You will see in a few days a Declaration setting forth the causes which have impelled us to this mighty revolution, and the reasons which will justify it in the sight of God and man. A plan of confederation will be taken up in a few days.

When I look back to the year 1761, and recollect the argument concerning writs of assistance in the superior court, which I have hitherto considered as the commencement of this controversy between Great Britain and America, and run through the whole period from that time to this, and recollect the series of political events, the chain of causes and effects, I am surprised at the suddenness as well as greatness of this revolution. Britain has been filled with folly, and America with wisdom. At least, this is my judgment. Time must determine.

It is the will of Heaven that the two countries should be sundered forever. It may be the will of Heaven that America shall suffer calamities still more wasting, and distress yet more dreadful. If this is to be the case, it will have this good effect at least. It will inspire us with many virtues which we have not and correct many errors, follies, and vices which threaten to disturb, dishonor and destroy us. The furnace of affliction produces refinement, in States as well as individuals.

And the new governments we are assuming in every part will require a purification from our vices, and an augmentation of our virtues, or they will be no blessings. The people will have unbounded power, and the people are extremely addicted to corruption and venality, as well as the great. But I must submit all my hopes and fears to an overruling Providence, in which, unfashionable as the faith may be, I firmly believe.

JOHN ADAMS TO ABIGAIL ADAMS:

3 July 1776

The second day of July, 1776, will be the most memorable Epocha in the history of America. I am apt to believe that it will be celebrated by succeeding generations as the great anniversary festival. It ought to be commemorated as the day of deliverance, by solemn acts of devotion to God Almighty. It ought to be solemnized with pomp and parade, with shows, games, sports, guns, bells, bonfires and illuminations, from one end of this continent to the other, from this time forward, forevermore.

You will think me transported with enthusiasm, but I am not. I am well aware of the toil, and blood, and treasure, that it will cost us to maintain this declaration, and support and defend these States. Yet, through all the gloom, I can see the rays of ravishing light and glory. I can see that the end is more than worth all the means, and that posterity will triumph in that day's transaction, even although we should rue it, which I trust in God we shall not.

The news of the signing in Philadelphia produced great excitement and enthusiasm throughout the colonies. A typical celebration, described in the following account, took place in Savannah, Georgia, on August 10, 1776. This report comes from Peter Force's collection of documents, *American Archives*.

His Excellency, the President, and the Honorable the Council met in the Council chamber, and read the Declaration. They then proceeded to the square before the Assembly House, and read it likewise before a great concourse of people, when the Grenadier and Light Infantry Companies fired a general volley. After this they proceeded in the following procession to the Liberty Pole: the Grenadiers in front; the Provost-Marshall on horseback, with his sword drawn; the Secretary with the Declaration; his Excellency the President; the Honorable the Council and Gentlemen; then the Light Infantry and the rest of the Militia of the town and district of Savannah.

At the Liberty Pole they were met by the Georgia Battalion who, after reading of the Declaration, discharged their field-pieces and fired in platoons. Upon this they proceeded to the Battery at the Trustees' garden, where the Declaration was read for the last time, and cannon of the Battery discharged. His Excellency and Council, Colonel Lachlan McIntosh, and other gentlemen, with the Militia, dined under the Cedar Trees, and cheerfully drank to the United Free and Independent States of America.

In the evening the town was illuminated, and there was exhibited a very solemn funeral procession, attended by the Grenadier and Light Infantry Companies, and other Militia, with their drums muffled and fifes, and a greater number of people than ever appeared on any occasion before in this Province, when George III was interred before the Court-House, in the following manner:

For as much as George III, of Great Britain, hath most flagrantly violated his coronation oath and trampled upon the constitution of our country and the sacred rights of mankind, we therefore commit his political existence to the ground, corruption to corruption, tyranny to the grave, and oppression to eternal infamy, in sure and certain hope that he will never obtain a resurrection to rule again over these United States of America. But my friends and fellow-citizens, let us not be sorry as men without hope for tyrants that thus depart; rather let us remember America is free and independent; that she is, and will be, with the blessing of the Almighty, great among the nations of the earth. Let this encourage us in well doing to fight for our rights and privileges, for our wives and children, for all that is near and dear unto us. May God give us His blessing, and let all the people say Amen!

THE PROBLEM OF THE LOYALIST

Public support of the Revolution was by no means universal. There were thousands upon thousands of loyalists in the colonies, many of whom were prosperous, solid citizens who had been community leaders. Some of them bore arms against the Continental Army; others went into voluntary or forced exile in Canada or England. Conducting the war was made more difficult by the presence of loyalists who at best were neutral, at worst were traitors. The following selections give a glimpse of this problem.

The first is by Michel-Guillaume Jean de Crevecoeur, a Frenchman who became a naturalized British subject and a farmer in New York State during the decade before the Revolution. De Crevecoeur had married an American girl and had prospered as an American farmer. He felt that he owed a great deal to King George and England. Thus when war came, he was torn between loyalty to the king and loyalty to his wife's people and his neighbors. He went back to Europe during the war, leaving his wife and children in America. De Crevecoeur's anguish is clearly shown in the following paragraphs from his book, *Letters from an American Farmer*, which he wrote under the name Hector St. John de Crevecoeur.

How easily do men pass from loving, to hating and cursing one another! I am a lover of peace, what must I do? I am divided between the respect I feel for the ancient connection, and the fear of innovations, with the consequence of which I am not well acquainted; as they are embraced by my own countrymen. I am conscious that I was happy before this unfortunate Revolution. I feel that I am no longer so; therefore I regret the change. This is the only mode of reasoning adapted to persons in my situation.

If I attach myself to the Mother Country, which is 3000 miles from me, I become what is called an enemy to my own region; if I follow the rest of my countrymen, I become opposed to our ancient masters: both extremes appear equally dangerous to a person of so little weight and consequence as I am, whose energy and example are of no avail. As to the argument on which the dispute is founded, I know little about it. Much has been said and written on both sides, but who has a judgment capacious and clear enough to decide? The great moving principles which actuate both parties are much hid from vulgar eyes, like mine; nothing but the plausible and the probable are offered to our contemplation....

Alas, how should I unravel an argument, in which reason herself hath given way to brutality and bloodshed! What then must I do? I ask the wisest lawyers, the ablest casuists [debaters], the warmest patriots; for I mean honestly. Great Source of wisdom! inspire me with light sufficient to guide my benighted steps out of this intricate maze! Shall I discard all my ancient principles, shall I renounce that name, that nation which I held once so respectable? . . .

Must I be called a parricide, a traitor, a villain, lose the esteem of all those whom I love, to preserve my own; be shunned like a rattlesnake, or be pointed at like a bear? I have neither heroism nor magnanimity enough to make so great a sacrifice.

Here I am tied, I am fastened by numerous strings, nor do I repine at the pressure they cause; ignorant as I am, I can pervade the utmost extent of the calamities which have already overtaken our poor afflicted country. I can see the great and accumulated ruin yet extending itself as far as the theatre of war has reached; I hear the groans of thousands of families now ruined and desolated by our aggressors. I cannot count the multitude of orphans this war has made; nor ascertain the immensity of blood we have lost.

Some have asked, whether it was a crime to resist; to repel some parts of this evil. Others have asserted, that a resistance so general makes pardon unattainable, and repentance useless; and dividing the crime among so many, renders it imperceptible. What one party calls meritorious, the other denominates flagitious [wicked]. These opinions vary, contract, or expand, like the events of the war on which they are founded. What can an insignificant man do in the midst of these jarring contradictory parties, equally hostile to persons situated as I am?

> The next selection describes the trials of a prominent Philadelphia doctor in August, 1775. This rough handling of Dr. Kearsley by the mob in Philadelphia was typical of the treatment given loyalists (usually called Tories) throughout the colonies. Not many loyalists were executed, as royalists were guillotined by the Jacobins during the French Revolution, but they suffered many indignities and often had their property confiscated. This account is from Alexander Graydon's *Memoirs*.

AMONG the disaffected in Philadelphia, Doctor Kearsley was pre-eminently ardent and rash. An extremely zealous Loyalist, and impetuous in his temper, he had given much umbrage to the whigs; and if I am not mistaken, he had been detected in some hostile machinations [dealings]. Hence he was deemed a proper subject for the fashionable punishment of tarring, feathering, and carting. He was seized at his own door by a party of the militia, and, in the attempt to resist them, received a wound in his hand from a bayonet. Being overpowered, he was placed in a cart provided for the purpose, and amidst a multitude of boys and idlers, paraded through the streets to the tune of the rogue's march. I happened to be at the coffeehouse when the concourse arrived there. They made a halt, while the Doctor, foaming with rage and indignation, without his hat, his wig dishevelled and bloody from his wounded hand, stood up in the cart and called for a bowl of punch. It was quickly handed to him; when so vehement was his thirst that he drained it of its contents before he took it from his lips.

What were the feelings of others on this lawless proceeding, I know not, but mine, I must confess, revolted at the spectacle. I was shocked at seeing a lately respected citizen so cruelly vilified, and was imprudent enough to say that, had I been a magistrate, I would, at every hazard, have interposed my authority in suppression of the outrage. But this was not the only instance which convinced me that I wanted nerves for a revolutionist. It must be admitted, however, that the conduct of the populace was marked by a lenity [gentleness] which peculiarly distinguished the cradle of our republicanism. Tar and feathers had been dispensed with, and excepting the injury he had received in his hand, no sort of violence was offered by the mob to their victim. But to a man of high spirit, as the Doctor was, the indignity in its lightest form was sufficient to madden him: it probably had this effect, since his conduct became so extremely outrageous that it was thought necessary to confine him. From the city he was soon after removed to Carlisle, where he died during the war.

The final selection dealing with the loyalists illustrates the problem from the side of the patriots. Here Sam Adams writes James Warren on February 16, 1777, describing the loyalists as more of a threat to America than the British army:

MY DEAR SIR,—A few days ago a small expedition was made by the authority of this State ;:tided by a detachment of Continental Regulars, to suppress the Tories in the Counties of Somerset and Worcester on the Eastern Shore of Chesapeake, where they are numerous and have arisen to a great pitch of violence. We this day have a rumour that one of their principals, a Doctor Cheyney, is taken and we hope to hear of the business being effectually done, very soon. In my opinion, much more is to be apprehended from the secret machinations of these rascally people than from the open violence of British and Hessian soldiers, whose success has been in a great measure owing to the aid they have received from them.

You know that the Tories in America have always acted upon one system. Their headquarters used to be at Boston—more lately at Philadelphia. They have continually embarrassed the public councils there and afforded intelligence, advice and assistance to General Howe. Their influence is extended throughout the United States. Boston has its full share of them, and yet I do not hear that measures have been taken to suppress them. On the contrary, I am informed that the citizens are grown so polite as to treat them with tokens of civility and respect. Can a man take fire into his bosom and not be burned? Your Massachusetts Tories communicate with the enemy in Britain as well as New York. They give and receive intelligence, from whence they early form a judgment of their measures. I am told they discovered an air of insolent triumph in their countenances, and saucily enjoyed the success of Howe's forces in Jersey before it happened.

Indeed, my friend, if measures are not soon taken, and the most vigorous ones, to root out these pernicious weeds, it will be in vain for America to persevere in this generous struggle for the public liberty.

III. The Major Battles and Trials

THE BATTLE OF LONG ISLAND

Excitement over the Declaration of Independence soon was tempered with the ominous news of British movements. In the North, following the failure of Arnold and Montgomery to capture Quebec in December, the American forces had been falling back steadily. By June they were back to Crown Point on the west shore of Lake Champlain. There was rejoicing when news circulated that Colonel Moultrie's makeshift fort of palmetto logs had thwarted British efforts to take Charleston, but this was the last good news for six months. The next news of British activities reported the imminent danger of New York City from invasion. General Washington faced the impossible task of defending the city with only seventeen thousand men. Lord Howe was camped on Staten Island with a vastly superior force.

In late August, Howe landed twenty thousand men, including Hessian mercenaries, at Gravesend Bay and prepared to attack the American fortifications, commanded by Israel Putnam, at Brooklyn Heights. The British were in a holiday mood as they disembarked. The following selection, which is from the journal of Howe's secretary, Ambrose Serie, describes the landing.

Thursday, August 22, 1776
EARLY this morning the English troops, the Highlanders and

Preston's Light Horse, landed on Long Island. The disembarkation was effected upon the flat shore, near Gravesend, without the least resistance; the inhuman Rebels contenting themselves with burning as much of the people's corn as they could (tho' the great rains which fell last night very happily prevented much of their design), with driving off their cattle as far as their time would permit, and doing as much injury to the inhabitants, who are generally well disposed, as they possibly could. The soldiers and sailors seemed as merry as in a holiday, and regaled themselves with the fine apples, which hung every where upon the trees in a great abundance. After the landing was pretty well effected, I went with two or three gentlemen on shore to Mr. De Nuys's house, opposite the Narrows, whose family were rejoiced at the deliverance from the tyranny they had so long undergone from the Rebels. It was really diverting to see sailors and apples tumbling from the trees together.

The General pushed on to his post, and was joined by great numbers of the people. Every thing relative to the disembarkation was conducted in admirable order, and succeeded beyond our most sanguine wishes.

The island seems extremely fertile, and the country rather flat. There were some fine cattle still remaining; and proper precautions were taken to prevent our people from plundering....

In a word, the disembarkation of about 15,000 troops, upon a fine beach, their forming upon the adjacent plain, a fleet of above 300 ships and vessels with their sails spread open to dry, the sun shining clear upon them, the green hills and meadows after the rain, and the calm surface of the water upon the contiguous sea and up the sound, exhibited one of the finest and most picturesque scenes that the imagination can fancy or the eye behold.

Add to all this the vast importance of the business and of the motions of the day, and the mind feels itself wonderfully engaged by the variety and greatness of the objects; but finds, or should find, in the midst of all, that there is no assurance or dependence in these things, but in Him only who saveth by many or by few, and who giveth the victory when and where and how He pleaseth. In this frame a man may be disappointed of his present wish, but not of his hope or future expectation. He may err in his judgment, but he is right in his heart.

> The battle was lost before it began. The British Highland regiments, moving along the coastal Gowanus Road, and the Hessians, on the direct Bedford and Flatbush roads, made contact with the American defenses on the morning of August 27th. A sharp, evenly matched battle began in this sector. But hardly had the issue been joined before General Sullivan, who faced the Hessians, was attacked from the rear by a larger force than he was already fighting. Three divisions under Cornwallis, Clinton, and Percy had slipped through an undefended pass in the hills east of Brooklyn and in a brilliant maneuver turned the American flank.
>
> Meantime, Lord Stirling, who commanded the American troops defending the Gowanus Road, fought four hours, then also was attacked from the rear. The battle became a rout, and the only question that remained was how many Americans could escape from the trap to reach the fortifications. Several thousand succeeded, some across the exposed salt marshes, but the American casualties by late afternoon stood at two thousand men killed, wounded, and captured, including two generals. The following selection summarizes the battle as seen by a British officer.

September 3, 1776

REJOICE, my friend, that we have given the Rebels a d——d crush. We landed on Long-Island the 22d ult., without opposition. On the 27th we had a very warm action, in which the Scots regiments behaved with the greatest bravery and carried the day after an obstinate resistance on the ·Rebel side. But we flanked and overpowered them with numbers. The Hessians and our brave Highlanders gave no quarters; and it was a fine sight to see with what alacrity they dispatched the Rebels with their bayonets after we had surrounded them so that they could not resist. Multitudes were drowned and suffocated in morasses—a proper punishment for all Rebels. Our battalion out-marched all the rest, and was always first up with the Rebel fugitives. A fellow they call Lord Stirling, one of their generals, with two others, is prisoner, and a great many of their officers, men, artillery, and stores. It was a glorious achievement, my friend, and will immortalize us and crush Rebel colonies. Our loss was nothing. We took care to tell the Hessians that the Rebels had resolved to give no quarters to them in particular, which made them fight desperately and put all to death that fell into their hands. You know all stratagems are lawful in war, especially against such vile enemies to their King and country. The island is all ours, and we shall soon take New-York, for the Rebels dare not look us in the face. I expect the affair will be over this campaign, and we shall all return covered with American laurels and have the cream of American lands allotted us for our services.

WASHINGTON'S RETREAT

Fortunately, Howe did not follow up this victory and attack the fortifications at Brooklyn Heights. Washington was able to evacuate his entire army from Brooklyn, and during the night of August 29 he collected every boat, sloop, yacht, fishing smock, yawl, scow, and rowboat he could lay his hands on. By seven A.M. the next morning the army had crossed the East River to Manhattan without losing a man. The American forces, however, could not hold Manhattan, and had to fall back slowly. Washington eventually had to retreat all the way across New Jersey into Pennsylvania, and by Christmas, 1776, the future of the infant United States looked very dismal.

At this dark moment, Thomas Paine again came to the aid of his adopted country, with a slim pamphlet that bolstered the sagging morale of the troops and the people. According to tradition, Paine wrote the first of a series of papers called The American Crisis by firelight on a drumhead. Washington had the pamphlet read to his troops. One week later the American army took the offensive, crossed the Delaware on Christmas night, and defeated the Hessians the following day. The following excerpts are from Paine's first pamphlet.

THESE are the times that try men's souls. The summer soldier and the sunshine patriot will, in this crisis, shrink from the service of his country; but he that stands it now, deserves the love and thanks of man and woman. Tyranny, like hell, is not easily conquered; yet we have this consolation with us, that the harder the conflict, the more glorious the triumph. What we obtain too cheap, we esteem too lightly: it is dearness only that gives every thing its value. Heaven knows how to put a proper price upon its goods; and it would be strange indeed if so celestial an article as FREEDOM should not be highly rated....

I have as little superstition in me as any man living, but my secret opinion has ever been, and still is, that God Almighty will not give up a people to military destruction, or leave them unsupportedly to perish, who have so earnestly and so repeatedly sought to avoid the calamities of war, by every decent method which wisdom could invent. Neither have I so much of the infidel in me, as to suppose that He has relinquished the government of the world, and given us up to the care of devils; and as I do not, I cannot see on what grounds the king of Britain can look up to heaven for help against us: a common murderer, a highwayman, or a house-breaker, has as good a pretense as he....

As I was with the troops at Fort Lee, and marched with them to the edge of Pennsylvania, I am well acquainted with many circumstances, which those who live at a distance know but little or nothing of. Our situation there was exceedingly cramped, the place being a narrow neck of land between the North River and the Hackensack. Our force was inconsiderable, being not one-fourth so great as Howe could bring against us. We had no army at hand to have relieved the garrison, had we shut ourselves up and stood on our defense. Our ammunition, light artillery, and the best part of our stores, had been removed, on the apprehension that Howe would endeavor to penetrate the Jerseys, in which case Fort Lee could be of no use to us....

We brought off as much baggage as the wagons could contain; the rest was lost. The simple object was to bring off the garrison, and march them on till they could be strengthened by the Jersey or Pennsylvania militia, so as to be enabled to make a stand. We stayed four days at Newark, collected our out-posts with some of the Jersey militia, and marched out twice to meet the enemy, on being informed that they were advancing, though our numbers were greatly inferior to theirs. Howe, in my little opinion, committed a great error in generalship in not throwing a body of forces off from Staten Island through Amboy, by which means he might have seized all our stores at Brunswick, and intercepted our march into Pennsylvania; but if we believe the power of hell to be limited, we must likewise believe that their agents are under some providential control.

I shall not now attempt to give all the particulars of our retreat to the Delaware; suffice it for the present to say, that both officers and men, though greatly harassed and fatigued, frequently without rest, covering, or provision, the inevitable consequences of a long retreat, bore it with a manly and martial spirit. All their wishes centred in one, which was, that the country would turn out and help them to drive the enemy back....

I turn with the warm ardor of a friend to those who have nobly stood, and are yet determined to stand the matter out: I call not upon a few, but upon all: not on *this* state or *that* state, but on *every* state: up and help us; lay your shoulders to the wheel; better have too much force than too little, when so great an object is at stake. Let it be told to the future world, that in the depth of winter, when nothing but hope and virtue could survive, that the city and the country, alarmed at one common danger, came forth to meet and to repulse it. Say not that thousands are gone, turn out your tens of thousands; throw not the burden of the day upon Providence, but *"show your faith by your works,"* that God may bless you.

It matters not where you live, or what rank of life you hold, the evil or the blessing will reach you all. The far and the near, the home counties and the back, the rich and the poor, will suffer or rejoice alike. The heart that feels not now is dead; the blood of his children will curse his cowardice, who shrinks back at a time when a little might have saved the whole, and made *them* happy. I love the man that can smile in trouble, that can gather strength from distress, and grow brave by reflection. 'Tis the business of little minds to shrink; but he whose heart is firm, and whose conscience approves his conduct, will pursue his principles unto death.

BURGOYNE'S SURRENDER AT SARATOGA

The year 1777 began with Washington's army taking the offensive in New Jersey. It closed with the surrender of General Burgoyne after the Battle of Saratoga. Burgoyne's defeat was the turning point in the war, although the Treaty of Paris was not signed for another six years. Great Britain's grand strategy to split the United States had failed. The victory for the Americans led directly to France's decision to come to the aid of the United States.

Burgoyne's plan had been to march down the Hudson River Valley to Albany, where he would be joined by troops under Col. Barry St. Leger, who was moving along the Mohawk River Valley. He originally had planned that Lord Howe would drive north from New York City to meet him. Thus New England would be cut off from the rest of the country. But instead, Howe sent his army to attack Pennsylvania. St. Leger's troops, meanwhile, were turned back at Fort Stanwix and forced to retreat to Canada.

The deeper Burgoyne penetrated into New York State, the longer and more precarious his supply lines became. When Howe failed to support him, his defeat became inevitable. General Gates' forces opposing Burgoyne began to receive reinforcements from nearby states; Burgoyne's forces began to dwindle. The climactic battles of Freeman's Farm and Bemis Heights at Saratoga were fought on September 19 and October 7. Burgoyne was decisively defeated. He then retreated a few miles under constant pursuit.

One of the best eyewitness accounts of Burgoyne's defeat and surrender was written by the Baroness Von Riedesel, wife of the Hessian General Riedesel, who fought under Burgoyne. In the following selection she tells what happened on October l o, six days before the British surrendered.

About two o'clock in the afternoon, the firing of cannon and small arms was again heard, and all was alarm and confusion. My husband sent me a message telling me to betake myself forthwith into a house which was not far from there. I seated myself in the calash [carriage] with my children, and had scarcely driven up to the house when I saw on the opposite side of the Hudson River five or six men with guns, which were aimed at us. Almost involuntarily threw the children on the bottom of the calash and myself over them. At the same instant the churls fired, and shattered the arm of a poor English soldier behind us, who was already wounded, and was also on the point of retreating into the house.

Immediately after our arrival a frightful cannonade began, principally directed against the house in which we had sought shelter, probably because the enemy believed, from seeing so many people flocking around it, that all the generals made it their headquarters. Alas! it harbored none but wounded soldiers, or women! We were finally obliged to take refuge in a cellar, in which I laid myself down in a corner not far from the door. My children lay down on the earth with their heads upon my lap, and in this manner we passed the entire night. A horrible stench, the cries of the children, and yet more than all this, my own anguish, prevented me from closing my eyes. On the following morning the cannonade again began, but from a different side. I advised all to go out of the cellar for a little while, during which time I would have it cleaned, as otherwise we would all be sick. They followed my suggestion, and I at once set many hands to work, which was in the highest degree necessary; for the women and children, being afraid to venture forth, had soiled the whole cellar.

After they had all gone out and left me alone, I for the first time surveyed our place of refuge. It consisted of three beautiful cellars, splendidly arched. I proposed that the most dangerously wounded of the officers should be brought into one of them; that the women should remain in another; and that all the rest should stay in the third, which was nearest the entrance. I had just given the cellars a good sweeping, and had fumigated them by sprinkling vinegar on burning coals, and each one had found his place prepared for him—when a fresh and terrible cannonade threw us all once more into alarm. Many persons, who had no right to come in, threw themselves against the door. My children were already under the cellar steps, and we would all have been crushed, if God had not given me strength to place myself before the door, and with extended arms prevent all from coming in; otherwise every one of us would have been severely injured.

Eleven cannon balls went through the house, and we could plainly hear them rolling over our heads. One poor soldier, whose leg they were about to amputate, having been laid upon a table for this purpose, had the other leg taken off by another cannon ball, in the very middle of the operation. His comrades all ran off, and when they again came back they found him in one corner of the room, where he had rolled in his anguish, scarcely breathing. I was more dead than alive, though not so much on account of our own danger as for that which enveloped my husband, who, however, frequently sent to see how I was getting along, and to tell me that he was still safe....

Our cook saw to our meals, but we were in want of water; and in order to quench thirst, I was often obliged to drink wine and give it, also, to the children. It was, moreover, the only thing that my husband could take, which fact so worked upon our faithful Rockel that he said to me one day, "I fear that the general drinks so much wine because he dreads falling into captivity, and is therefore weary of life." The continual danger in which my husband was encompassed was a constant source of anxiety to me. I was the only one of all the women whose husband had not been killed or wounded, and I often said to myself—especially since my husband was placed in such great danger day and night—"Shall I be the only fortunate one?" He never came into the tent at night, but lay outside by the watch fires. This alone was sufficient to have caused his death, as the nights were damp and cold.

As the great scarcity of water continued, we at last found a soldier's wife who had the courage to bring water from the river, for no one else would undertake it, as the enemy shot at the head of every man who approached the river. This woman, however, they never molested; and they told us afterward that they spared her on account of her sex.

I endeavored to divert my mind from my troubles by constantly busying myself with the wounded. I made them tea and coffee, and received in return a thousand benedictions. Often, also, I shared my noonday meal with them. One day a Canadian officer came into our cellar who could scarcely stand up. We at last got it out of him that he was almost dead with hunger. I considered myself very fortunate to have it in my power to offer him my mess. This gave him renewed strength, and gained· for me his friendship. Afterward, upon our return to Canada, I learned to know his family. One of our greatest annoyances was the stench of the wounds when they began to suppurate.

VALLEY FORGE

War is by no means all battles and action. There are dull stretches of garrison life in between, and during the Revolution the dullness was accompanied by misery. Despite the American victory over Burgoyne at Saratoga, the following winter was a time of trial for Washington's army in its camp at Volley Forge. The army suffered every kind of shortage and privation. Meantime, the British in nearby Philadelphia were snugly holed up for the winter in the provisional capital of the United States.

The following selections give a glimpse of the army during that terrible winter. The first is from the journal of Private James Martin, who described the army's condition just before it took up winter quarters at Valley Forge. The second is from the diary of Surgeon Albigence Waldo and was written just after he reached the winter quarters.

FROM PRIVATE JAMES MARTIN'S JOURNAL:
THE army was now not only starved but naked; the greatest part were not only shirtless and barefoot, but destitute of all other clothing, especially blankets. I procured a small piece of raw cowhide and made myself a pair of moccasins, which kept my feet (while they lasted) from the frozen ground, although, as I well remember, the hard edges so galled my ankles, while on a march, that it was with much difficulty and pain that I could wear them afterwards; but the only alternative I had was to endure this inconvenience or to go barefoot, as hundreds of my companions had to, till they might be tracked by their blood upon the rough frozen ground. But hunger, nakedness and sore shins were not the only difficulties we had at that time to encounter; we had hard duty to perform and little or no strength to perform it with.

The army continued at and near the Gulf for some days, after which we marched for the Valley Forge in order to take up our winter-quarters. We were now in a truly forlorn condition—no clothing, no provisions and as disheartened as need be. We arrived, however, at our destination a few days before Christmas. Our prospect was indeed dreary. In our miserable condition, to go into the wild woods and build us habitations to stay (not to live) in, in such a weak, starved and naked condition, was appalling in the highest degree, especially to New-Englanders, unaccustomed to such kind of hardships at home.

FROM SURGEON ALBIGENCE WALDO'S DIARY:
December 21.—[*Valley Forge.*] PREPARATIONS made for huts. Provisions scarce. Mr. Ellis went homeward—sent a letter to my wife. Heartily wish myself at home. My skin and eyes are almost spoiled with continual smoke. A general cry thro' the camp this evening among the soldiers, "No meat! No meat!" The distant vales echoed back the melancholy sound—"No meat! No meat!" Imitating the noise of crows and owls, also, made a part of the confused music.

What have you for your dinners, boys? "Nothing but fire cake and water, Sir." At night: "Gentlemen, the supper is ready." What is your supper, lads? "Fire cake and water, Sir."

Very poor beef has been drawn in our camp the greater part of this season. A butcher bringing a quarter of this kind of beef into camp one day who had white buttons on the knees of his breeches, a soldier cries out: "There, there, Tom, is some more of your fat beef. By my soul I can see the butcher's breeches buttons through it."

December 22.—Lay excessive cold and uncomfortable last night. My eyes are started out from their orbits like a rabbit's eyes, occasioned by a great cold and smoke.

What have you got for breakfast, lads? "Fire cake and water, Sir." The Lord send that our Commissary of Purchases may live [on] fire cake and water till their glutted guts are turned to pasteboard.

Our division are under marching orders this morning. I am ashamed to say it, but .I am tempted to steal fowls if I could find them, or even a whole hog, for I feel as if I could eat one. But the impoverished country about us affords but little matter to employ a thief, or keep a clever fellow in good humour. But why do I talk of hunger and hard usage, when so many in the world have not even fire cake and water to eat?

JOHN PAUL JONES DEFEATS THE *SERAPIS*

As we have seen, the war began in New England and eventually spread to the Middle Atlantic states. It also was fought at sea where the odds against the Americans were even greater than on land. At the beginning of the war, the United States had no navy, whereas England's fleet was the best in the world. Yet the infant American navy managed to harass British shipping, win some important battles, and even carry the war to England in coastal raids. It was like a tough little terrier snapping at the heels of a burglar—not able to save the family silver but enough of a nuisance to interrupt the robbery.

The exploits of John Paul Jones have been recounted many times in song and story. His victory over the British warship *Serapis* is an exciting tale, and in the following selection one of his officers, Lt. Richard Dale, reports the battle. This action occurred off the coast of England on September 23, 1779. The battle began when Jones sighted a convoy of 40 English merchant ships under the escort of the *Serapis*.

AT this moment I received orders from Commodore Jones to commence the action with a broadside, which indeed appeared to be simultaneous on board both ships. Our position being to windward of the *Serapis* we passed ahead of her, and the *Serapis* coming up on our larboard quarter, the action commenced abreast of each other. The *Serapis* soon passed ahead of the *Bon Homme Richard,* and when he thought he had gained a distance sufficient to go down athwart the fore foot to rake us, found he had not enough distance, and that the *Bon Homme Richard* would be aboard him, put his helm a-lee, which brought the two ships on a line, and the *Bon Homme Richard*, having head way, ran her bows into the stern of the *Serapis*.

We had remained in this situation but a few minutes when we were again hailed by the *Serapis*, "Has your ship struck?"

To which Captain Jones answered, "I have not yet begun to fight!"

As we were unable to bring a single gun to bear upon the *Serapis* our topsails were backed, while those of the *Serapis* being filled, the ships separated. The *Serapis* bore short round upon her heel, and her jibboom ran into the mizen rigging of the *Bon Homme Richard*. In this situation the ships were made fast together with a hawser, the bowsprit of the *Serapis* to the mizenmast of the *Bon Homme Richard*, and the action recommenced from the starboard sides of the two ships....

The fire from the tops of the *Bon Homme Richard* was conducted with so much skill and effect as to destroy ultimately every man who appeared upon the quarter-deck of the *Serapis*, and induced her commander to order the survivors to go below. Nor even under the shelter of the decks were they more secure. The powder-monkeys of the *Serapis*, finding no officer to receive the 18-pound cartridges brought from the magazines, threw them on the main deck and went for more.

These cartridges being scattered along the deck and numbers of them broken, it so happened that some of the hand-grenades thrown from the main-yard of the *Bon Homme Richard*, which was directly over the main-hatch of the *Serapis*, fell upon this powder and produced a most awful explosion. The effect was tremendous; more than twenty of the enemy were blown to pieces, and many stood with only the collars of their shirts upon their bodies. In less than an hour afterward, the flag of England, which had been nailed to the mast of the *Serapis*, was struck by Captain Pearson's own hand, as none of his people would venture aloft on this duty; and this too when more than 1500 persons [on shore] were witnessing the conflict, and the humiliating termination of it, from Scarborough and Flamborough Head.

Upon finding that the flag of the Serapis had been struck, I went to Captain Jones and asked whether I might board the *Serapis,* to which he consented, and jumping upon the gun-wale, seized the main-brace pennant and swung myself upon her quarter-deck. Midshipman Mayrant followed with a party of men and was immediately run through the thigh with a boarding pike by some of the enemy stationed in the waist, who were not informed of the surrender of their ship.

I found Captain Pearson standing on the leeward side of the quarter-deck and, addressing myself to him, said, "Sir, I have orders to send you on board the ship alongside." The first lieutenant of the *Serapis* coming up at this moment inquired of Captain Pearson whether the ship alongside had struck to him. To which I replied, "No, Sir, the contrary: he has struck to us."

The lieutenant renewed his inquiry, "Have you struck, Sir?"

"Yes, I have."

BENEDICT ARNOLD'S TREASON

Among the infamous traitors of history, Benedict Arnold has few peers. His attempt to surrender West Point to the British in 1780 and the capture and execution of Major Andre are well-known stories. They make up the most exciting cloak-and-dagger episode of the entire Revolution and have all the elements of high drama. Arnold had served his country brilliantly al Quebec, on Lake Champlain, and at Saratoga, and as a major general he was one of Washington's most trusted officers. Major Andre was a dashing, handsome young British officer whose capture in civilian clothes (which technically made him a spy) was accidental. Historians never have fully decided what made Arnold betray his country, but betray it he did, and he escaped to be rewarded by the British government. Major Andre, who was only the go-between, was caught and hanged. The following selections describe these events vividly. The first is a letter the Marquis de Lafayette wrote to the Chevalier de la Luzerne, France's minister to the United States. The second is Dr. James Thacher's eyewitness account of Andre's execution.

LAFAYETTE TO THE CHEVALIER DE LA LUZERNE:

West Point, 25 September 1780

WHEN I left you yesterday morning, M. le Chevalier, to come here to take breakfast with General Arnold, we were very far from thinking of the event which I am now about to announce to you. You will shudder at the danger we have run. You will be astonished at the miraculous chain of accidents and circumstances by which we have been saved. But you will be still more greatly surprised when you learn by what instrument this conspiracy was being carried on. West Point was sold, and it was sold by Arnold!

That same man who had covered himself with glory by rendering valuable services to his country, had lately formed a horrid compact with the enemy. And, but for the chance which brought us here at a certain time, but for the chance which, by a combination of accidents, caused the Adjutant-General of the English army to fall into the hands of some countrymen, beyond the line of our own posts, West Point and the North River would probably be in the possession of our enemies.

When we left Fishkill we were preceded by one of my aides-de-camp and General Knox's aide, who found General and Mrs. Arnold at table and who sat down to breakfast with them. During that time two letters were brought to General Arnold giving him information of the capture of the spy. He ordered a horse saddled, went to his wife's room and told her that he was lost, and directed one of his aides-de-camp to say to General Washington that he had gone to West Point and should return in an hour.

Upon our arrival here, we crossed the river and went to look at the works. Judge our astonishment when, upon our return, we were informed that the captured spy was Major Andre, the Adjutant General of the English army, and that among the papers found upon him was a copy of a very important council of war, a statement of the strength of the garrison and of the works, and certain observations upon the methods of attack and defense, all in General Arnold's handwriting. The English Adjutant-General wrote also to the General, admitting his rank and his name.

A search was made for Arnold, but he had escaped in a boat on board the sloop of war Vulture, and, as nobody suspected his flight, no sentry could have thought of arresting him. Colonel Hamilton...who had gone in quest of Arnold, received soon afterward a flag of truce with a letter from Arnold for the General, in which he made no effort to justify his treason, and a letter from the English Commandant, Robinson, who in a most insolent manner demanded the surrender of the Adjutant-General, upon the ground that he had been acting under the permission of General Arnold.

DOCTOR JAMES THACHER DESCRIBES ANDRE'S EXECUTION:
October 2d, 1780.—MAJOR Andre is no more among the living. I have just witnessed his exit. 1t was a tragical scene of the deepest interest. During his confinement and trial, he exhibited those proud and elevated sensibilities which designate greatness and dignity of mind. Not a murmur or a sigh ever escaped him, and the civilities and attentions bestowed on him were politely acknowledged. Having left a mother and two sisters in England, he was heard to mention them in terms of the tenderest affection, and in his letter to Sir Henry Clinton he recommended them to his particular attention.

The principal guard officer, who was constantly in the room with the prisoner, relates that when the hour of his execution was announced to him in the morning, he received it without emotion, and while all present were affected with silent gloom, he retained a firm countenance, with calmness and composure of mind. Observing his servant enter the room in tears, he exclaimed, "Leave me till you can show yourself more manly!" His breakfast being sent to him from the table of General Washington, which had been done every day of his confinement, he partook of it as usual, and having shaved and dressed himself, he placed his hat on the table and cheerfully said to the guard officers, "I am ready at any moment, gentlemen, to wait on you."

The fatal hour having arrived, a large detachment of troops was paraded, and an immense concourse of people assembled; almost all our general and field officers, excepting His Excellency and his staff, were present on horseback; melancholy and gloom pervaded all ranks, and the scene was affectingly awful. I was so near during the solemn march to the fateful spot as to observe every movement and participate in every emotion which the melancholy scene was calculated to produce. Major Andre walked from the stone house, in which he had been confined, between two of our subaltern officers, arm in arm. The eyes of the immense multitude were fixed on him, who, rising superior to the fears of death, appeared as if conscious of the dignified deportment which he displayed. He betrayed no want of fortitude, but retained a complacent smile on his countenance, and politely bowed to several gentlemen whom he knew, which was respectfully returned.

It was his earnest desire to be shot, as being the mode of death most conformable to the feelings of a military man, and he had indulged the hope that his request would be granted. At the moment, therefore, when suddenly he came in view of the gallows, he involuntarily started backward and made a pause.

"Why this emotion, sir?" said an officer by his side.

Instantly recovering his composure, he said, "I am reconciled to my death, but I detest the mode."

While waiting and standing near the gallows, I observed some degree of trepidation: placing his foot on a stone and rolling it over, and choking in his throat as if attempting to swallow. So soon, however, as he perceived that things were in readiness, he stepped quickly into the wagon, and at this moment he appeared to shrink, but instantly elevating his head with firmness, he said, "It will be but a momentary pang," and taking from his pocket two white handkerchiefs, the provost-marshal, with one, loosely pinioned his arms, and with the other, the victim, after taking off his hat and stock, bandaged his own eyes with perfect firmness, which melted the hearts and moistened the cheeks, not only of his servant, but of the throng of spectators.

THE END OF THE WAR: YORKTOWN

More than six years after the first shot was fired at Lexington, the long struggle came to an end in the South. After the British were defeated at Saratoga and Lord Howe was replaced by Sir Henry Clinton in command of British forces in the New York-Philadelphia area, England turned her attention to the southern states. There the British had more success. They defeated the Americans in one battle after another, occupied Georgia and South Carolina, and pushed into North Carolina. By the time of Arnold's treachery, America's prospects everywhere looked dismal.

General Washington then shook up his command and replaced General Gates in the South with General Greene. Lafayette, meantime, had gone home to France and persuaded his government to send an army to help the hard-pressed Americans. In 1781 these troops under an experienced soldier, the Count de Rochambeau, and a French fleet commanded by Count de Grasse, joined the American forces as Lord Cornwallis moved into Virginia. When the British commander made his comp at Yorktown, Washington and the French fleet were able to cut off his escape either by land or sea. The last phase of the war was the siege of Cornwallis' army, and for a glimpse of this final chapter in the military record of the Revolution, we again call on Dr. Thacher's journal. The surrender of Cornwallis took place on October 19, 1781.

From the 10th to the 15th a tremendous and incessant firing from the American and French batteries is kept up, and the enemy return the fire, but with little effect. A red-hot shell from the French battery set fire to the Charon, a British 44-gun ship, and two or three smaller vessels at anchor in the river, which were consumed in the night. From the bank of the river I had a fine view of this splendid conflagration. The ships were enwrapped in a torrent of fire, which, spreading with vivid brightness among the combustible rigging, and running with amazing rapidity to the tops of the several masts, while all around was thunder and lightning from our numerous cannon and mortars, and in the darkness of night, presented one of the most sublime and magnificent spectacles which can be imagined. Some of our shells, overreaching the town, are seen to fall into the river and, bursting, throw up columns of water like the spouting of the monsters of the deep.

We have now made further approaches to the town by throwing up a second parallel line and batteries within about three hundred yards; this was effected in the night, and at day-light the enemy were roused to the greatest exertions; the engines of war have raged with redoubled fury and destruction on both sides, no cessation day or night....

The siege is daily becoming more and more formidable and alarming, and his lordship must view his situation as extremely critical, if not desperate. Being in the trenches every other night and day, I have a fine opportunity of witnessing the sublime and stupendous scene which is continually exhibiting. The bombshells from the besiegers and the besieged are incessantly crossing each others' path in the air. They are clearly visible in the form of a black ball in the day, but in the night they appear like a fiery meteor with a blazing tail, most beautifully brilliant, ascending majestically from the mortar to a certain altitude and gradually descending to the spot where they are destined to execute their work of destruction.

It is astonishing with what accuracy an experienced gunner will make his calculations, that a shell shall fall within a few feet of a given point, and burst at the precise time, though at a great distance. When a shell falls, it whirls round, burrows, and excavates the earth to a considerable extent and, bursting, makes dreadful havoc around. I have more than once witnessed fragments of the mangled bodies and limbs of the British soldiers thrown into the air by the bursting of our shells; and by one from the enemy, Captain White, of the Seventh Massachusetts Regiment, and one soldier were killed and another wounded near where I was standing....

The enemy having two redoubts, about three hundred yards in front of their principal works, which enfiladed [raked with gunfire] our intrenchment and impeded our approaches, it was resolved to take possession of them both by assault. The one on the left of the British garrison, bordering on the banks of the river, was assigned to our brigade of light-infantry, under the command of the Marquis de Lafayette. The advanced corps was led on by the intrepid Colonel Hamilton, who had commanded a regiment of light-infantry during the campaign, and assisted by Colonel Gimat.

The assault commenced at eight o'clock in the evening, and the assailants bravely entered the fort with the point of the bayonet without firing a single gun. We suffered the loss of eight men killed and about thirty wounded, among whom Colonel Gimat received a slight wound in his foot, and Major Gibbs, of his excellency's guard, and two other officers were slightly wounded. Major Campbell, who commanded in the fort, was wounded and taken prisoner, with about thirty soldiers; the remainder made their escape. I was desired to visit the wounded in the fort even before the balls had ceased whistling about my ears, and saw a sergeant and eight men dead in the ditch. A captain of our infantry, belonging to New Hampshire, threatened to take the life of Major Campbell to avenge the death of his favorite, Colonel Shammel; but Colonel Hamilton interposed, and not a man was killed after he ceased to resist.

During the assault, the British kept up an incessant firing of cannon and musketry from their whole line. His Excellency General

Washington, Generals Lincoln and Knox, with their aids, having dismounted, were standing in an exposed situation waiting the result.

Colonel Cobb, one of General Washington's aids, solicitous for his safety, said to His Excellency, "Sir, you are too much exposed here. Had you not better step a little back?"

"Colonel Cobb," replied His Excellency, "if you are afraid, you have liberty to step back."

IV. Winning the Peace

NEGOTIATIONS AND REFLECTIONS

The surrender of Lord Cornwallis at Yorktown did not force England to make peace. The British still had a large army in the United States, and if Parliament had thought the war worth continuing, England certainly could have done so. However, the British government realized that it could not stamp out the rebellion, and many Englishmen were unwilling, if not downright opposed, to prolonging the hostilities. In addition, England was now at war in Europe and in other parts of the world against France, Spain, and the Netherlands. Most of the other nations of Europe had joined in a League of Armed Neutrality, which hampered Britain's naval measures against her enemies. Faced with a prolonged world war, England wanted peace.

British emissaries began putting out peace feelers in 1782, but it wasn't until the following year that the Peace of Paris was signed. Treaty negotiations for the United States were carried out by Benjamin Franklin, John Jay, and John Adams, who managed to obtain a better treaty than the Americans had ever expected. In fact, the accomplishment of the peace commissioners was a masterpiece of diplomacy. Not only was England reluctant to grant complete independence and territory all the way to the Mississippi, but France and her ally Spain did not want a large, independent nation in North America.

The French government brought pressure on Congress to instruct the commissioners to let France help negotiate the treaty. Thus Franklin, Adams, and Jay had to keep their treaty talks secret from their French allies, while at the same time insisting that the British negotiators make concessions they were reluctant to grant. In the five selections that follow, we have collected significant letters by the three commissioners about the treaty negotiations. The first two are by John Adams and John Jay, both written in the fall of 1782 to Robert Livingston, Secretary of Foreign Affairs.

JOHN ADAMS TO ROBERT LIVINGSTON:
I SET off for Paris, where I arrived on Saturday, the 26th of this month, after a tedious journey, the roads being, on account of long-continued rains, in the worst condition I ever knew them.

I waited forthwith on Mr. Jay, and from him learned the state of the conferences. It is not possible at present to enter into details. All I can say is, in general, that I had the utmost satisfaction in finding that he had been all along acting here upon the same principles upon which I had ventured to act in Holland, and that we were perfectly agreed in our sentiments and systems. I can not express it better than in his own words: "to be honest and grateful to our allies, but to think for ourselves."

I find a construction put upon one article of our instructions by some persons which, I confess, I never put upon it myself. It is represented by some as subjecting us to the French ministry, as taking away from us all right of judging for ourselves, and obliging us to agree to whatever the French ministers should advise us to do, and to do nothing without their consent. I never supposed this to be the intention of Congress; if I had, I never would have accepted the commission, and if I now thought it their intention I could not continue in it. I can not think it possible to be the design of Congress; if it is I hereby resign my place in the commission, and request that another person may be immediately appointed in my stead.

Yesterday we met Mr. Oswald at his lodgings; Mr. Jay, Dr. Franklin and myself on one side, and Mr. Oswald, assisted by Mr. Strachey, a gentleman whom I had the honor to meet in company with Lord Howe upon Staten Island in the year 1776, and assisted also by a Mr. Roberts, a clerk in some of the public offices, with books, maps and papers relative to the boundaries.

I arrived in a lucky moment for the boundary of Massachusetts, because I brought with me all the essential documents relative to that object, which are this day to be laid before my colleagues in conference at my house, and afterwards before Mr. Oswald.

It is now apparent, at least to Mr. Jay and myself, that in order to obtain the western lands, the navigation of the Mississippi, and the fisheries, or any of them, we must act with firmness and independence, as well as prudence and delicacy. With these there is little doubt we may obtain them all.

JOHN JAY TO ROBERT LIVINGSTON:
THESE are critical times, and great necessity there is for prudence and secrecy.

So far, and in such matters as this court [the French officials] may think it their interest to support us, they certainly will, but no further, in my opinion.

They are interested in separating us from Great Britain, and on that point we may, I believe, depend upon them; but it is not their interest that we should become a great and formidable people, and therefore they will not help us to become so.

It is not their interest that such a treaty should be formed between us and Britain as would produce cordiality and mutual confidence. They will therefore endeavor to plant such seeds of jealousy, discontent and discord in it as may naturally and perpetually keep our eyes fixed on France for security. This consideration must induce them to wish to render Britain formidable in our neighborhood, and to leave us as few resources of wealth and power as possible.

It is their interest to keep some point or other in contest between us and Britain to the end of the war, to prevent the possibility of our sooner agreeing, and thereby keep us employed in the war, and dependent on them for supplies. Hence they have favored and will continue to favor the British demands as to matters of boundary and the Tories.

The same views will render them desirous to continue the war in our country as long as possible, nor do I believe they will take any measures for our repossession of New York unless the certainty of its evacuation should render such an attempt advisable. The Count de Vergennes lately said that there could be no great use in expeditions to take places which must be given up to us at a peace.

Such being our situation, it appears to me advisable to keep up our army to the end of the war, even if the enemy should evacuate our country; nor does it appear to me prudent to listen to any overtures for carrying a part of it to the West Indies in case of such an event.

I think we have no rational dependence except on God and ourselves, nor can I yet be persuaded that Great Britain has either wisdom, virtue or magnanimity enough to adopt a perfect and liberal system of conciliation. If they again thought they could conquer us, they would again attempt it....

It is not my meaning, and therefore I hope I shall not be understood to mean, that we should deviate in the least from our treaty with France; our honor and our interest are concerned in inviolably adhering to it. I mean only to say that if we lean on her love of liberty, her affection for America, or her disinterested magnanimity, we shall lean on a broken reed, that will sooner or later pierce our hands.

———•———

The last three selections contain an exchange of letters between Franklin and the Count de Vergennes, the French Foreign Minister. Franklin's soothing letter explaining the commissioners' failure to consult France about the treaty is a marvelous bit of diplomacy. Imagine calling the deliberate withholding of the treaty terms until the treaty was completed a mere "indiscretion"! The last letter is Franklin's final comment on the end of the Revolution, written to Sir Joseph Banks, president of the most important scientific society of the day, the British Royal Society.

THE COUNT DE VERGENNES TO FRANKLIN:

Versailles, December 15, 1782

I AM at a loss, sir, to explain your conduct and that of your colleagues on this occasion. You have concluded your preliminary articles without any communication between us, although the instructions from Congress prescribe that nothing shall be done without the participation of the King. You are about to hold out a certain hope of peace to America without even informing yourself on the state of the negotiation on our part.

You are wise and discreet, sir; YQU perfectly understand what is due to propriety; you have all your life performed your duties. I pray you to consider how you propose to fulfill those which are due to the King. I am not desirous of enlarging these reflections; I commit them to your own integrity. When you shall be pleased to relieve my uncertainty I will entreat the King to enable me to answer your demands.

FRANKLIN TO THE COUNT DE VERGENNES:

Passy, December 17, 1782

NOTHING has been agreed in the preliminaries contrary to the interests of France; and no peace is to take place between us and England till you have concluded yours. Your observation is, however, apparently just, that in not consulting you before they were signed, we have been guilty of neglecting a point of *bienséance* [proper conduct]. But as this was not from want of respect to the King, whom we all love and honor, we hope it will be excused, and that the great work, which has hitherto been so happily conducted, is so nearly brought to perfection, and is so glorious to his reign, will not be ruined by a single indiscretion of ours. And certainly the whole edifice sinks to the ground immediately if you refuse on that account to give us any further assistance.

We have not yet dispatched the ship, and I beg leave to wait upon you on Friday for an answer.

It is not possible for any one to be more sensible than I am of what I and every American owe to the King for the many and great benefits and favors he has bestowed upon us. All my letters to America are proofs of this; all tending to make the same impressions on the minds of my countrymen that I felt in my own. And I believe that no prince was ever more beloved and respected by his own subjects than the King is by the people of the United States. *The English, I just now learn, flatter themselves they have already divided us.* I hope this little misunderstanding will therefore be kept a secret, and that they will find themselves totally mistaken.

FRANKLIN TO SIR JOSEPH BANKS:

Passy, July 27, 1783

I JOIN with you most cordially in rejoicing at the return of peace. I hope it will be lasting, and that mankind will at length, as they call themselves reasonable creatures, have reason and sense enough to settle their differences without cutting throats; for, in my opinion, *there never was a good war or a bad peace.* What vast additions to the conveniences and comforts of living might mankind have acquired, if the money spent in wars had been employed in works of public utility! What an extension of agriculture, even to the tops of our mountains; what rivers rendered navigable or joined by canals; what bridges, aqueducts, new roads and other public works, edifices and improvements, rendering England a complete paradise, might have been obtained by spending those millions in doing good which in the last war have been spent in doing mischief; in bringing misery into thousands of families, and destroying the lives of so many thousands of working people, who might have performed the useful labor!

PART THREE

The Age of Washington
1783-1801

Preface

After the Revolutionary War ended and the peace treaty had been signed, the United States was a nation in name only. The thirteen states that had carried out a successful rebellion against England still had the enormous problem of forming a stable and enduring government. One might think that fighting a war would be harder than writing a constitution and getting it adopted, but the historical record provides little support for this idea. The fact is that people can forget their differences in times of physical danger, and from Lexington to Yorktown the military operations of the British army furnished an overwhelming reason for Americans to unite.

From the end of the war until 1787, however, the United States passed through a period of reaction and transition. States were jealous of their sovereignty and refused to be governed by a central authority. This was the period of the Articles of Confederation, an unhappy era of national growing pains. Congress during these years was so weak that it had to go hat in hand, begging the states to give it money to operate the government.

Eventually, responsible statesmen throughout the United States realized that a strong central government was a necessity if the nation was to survive. The only alternative seemed to be thirteen separate countries. Hence leaders in the various states called a constitutional convention in Philadelphia in the summer of 1787; and during that historic summer, they drafted a constitution that has served as our basic law ever since. In due course of time, the states ratified the Constitution, and the new government came into existence.

Next followed the inauguration and administration of George Washington, whose name we have given to the entire era covered by this booklet. The young nation prospered under the leadership of Washington; and though the problems of banking, finance, taxation, and foreign affairs vexed Congress, the new Constitution was adequate to meet the challenge. Later, after Washington retired to Mt. Vernon and John Adams succeeded him as our second President, the nation was sharply divided over foreign events, chiefly conflicts with France, and partisan political battles made the last four years of the 1790s a turbulent period.

The selections in this booklet illustrate all of these problems and events in the formative years of the republic. They begin with some glimpses of life in the United States in the postwar period and then go on to document the period of the Confederation, the Constitutional Convention, and the administrations of Washington and Adams. We not only have used the great figures of the period, Hamilton, Jefferson, Adams, and Madison, to tell the story, but we also have coiled on a host of the minor actors in the drama.

In editing the manuscripts in this booklet, we have followed the practice of modernizing punctuation, capitalization, and spelling only when necessary to make the selections clear. We have silently corrected misspelled words and typographical errors. Wherever possible, we have used complete selections, but occasionally space limitations made necessary cuts in the original documents. Such cuts are indicated by spaced periods. In general, the selections appear as the authors wrote them.

Richard B. Morris
James Woodress

I. Life in America After the Revolution

EMIGRATION REPORTS

Peace and independence provided a powerful stimulus for American growth. Between 1790 and 1800 the population of the United States increased a third, as Europeans left the Old World to start life over in the new republic. Many of the newcomers pushed across the Allegheny Mountains to the Ohio Valley; some stayed in the cities. For a long time, however, the United States remained a nation of farmers; and, with the addition of Baltimore, the same cities which had been important commercial centers before the Revolution remained the only significant urban areas. Travelers and natives who wrote about America in this period saw the country as a land of promise, though often the promise was yet to be realized.

Brissot de Warville's Travels

Brissot de Warville was a young French journalist who visited the United States in 1788 and then went home to take an active part in the French Revolution. His account of the United States during the period of the Confederation is a fascinating report, but it is not very objective. Brissot was acutely aware of the contrasts between the decaying social order in France on the eve of revolution and the youthful vigor of America. He looks at the United States through rose-colored glasses and makes excuses for the unattractive features of American life that he sees. In the following selection, he describes his journey through Connecticut to New York. His book, which was translated into English in 1792, was published in London as *New Travels in the United States*. [The translation that follows is by the editors.]

THE environs of Hartford display a charming cultivated country; neat elegant houses, vast meadows covered with herds of cattle of an enormous size which furnish the market of New York and even Philadelphia. One sees sheep resembling ours, but not like ours, watched by shepherds or tormented by dogs. One sees sows of a prodigious size surrounded with numerous families of pigs, wearing on their necks a triangular piece of wood invented to hinder them from passing the barriers which enclose the cultivated fields. Turkeys and geese are abundant as well as potatoes and other vegetables: thus commodities of every kind are excellent and cheap. There the fruit alone does not partake of this universal bounty because it is less attended to. Peaches are abundant there but not good. Apples are used for making cider, and great quantities of them are shipped away.

To describe the neighborhood of Hartford is to describe Connecticut....Nature and art here display all their treasures; it is really the paradise of the United States....This state owes all its advantages to its situation. It is a fertile plain enclosed between two mountains, which render difficult its communications by land with the nearby states, [and] which consequently remove fears and dangers. It is watered by the superb Connecticut River, which flows into the sea and whose navigation is especially safe and easy. Agriculture being the basis of the wealth of this state, the wealth is more equally divided. There is more equality, less misery, more simplicity, more virtue, more of everything which constitutes republicanism.

Connecticut appears like one continuous town. On quitting Hartford, we entered Wethersfield, a town which is no less attractive: very spread out and full of well-built houses....Wethersfield is remarkable for its vast fields, uniformly covered with onions, great quantities of which are exported to the West Indies, and by its elegant meetinghouse or church. They say that on Sundays it offers an enchanting spectacle in the number of young and handsome persons who assemble there and by the agreeable music with which they intersperse the divine service.

New Haven yields not to Wethersfield in the beauty of the girls. At balls during the winter, despite the Puritan rigidity, it is not rare to see a hundred charming girls adorned with those brilliant complexions seldom met with when one journeys towards the South, and dressed with elegant simplicity.

The beauty of good breeding is equally striking in all of Connecticut's numerous population. You do not go into a tavern without meeting there above all propriety, decency, and dignity. The tables often are served by a young girl, respectable and pretty; by an amiable mother, whose age has not affected the agreeableness of her features and who retains her youth; by men who have that air of dignity which gives the idea of equality and who are not ignoble and base like most of our own tavern keepers.

On the road you often come upon those fair Connecticut girls either driving a carriage or galloping boldly alone on horseback and wearing fine hats, white aprons, and calico gowns, practices which prove at the same time the early development of their minds, since they are entrusted so young alone to the safety of the roads and the general innocence. You meet girls hazarding themselves alone without chaperons in the public stagecoaches. I am wrong to say hazarding. Who can offend them? They are here under the protection of public morals and of their own innocence. It is the consciousness of this innocence which rends them so obliging and so good; for a stranger takes them by the hand, clasps it, and laughs with them without their being. offended by it.

If one wants still more proofs of the prosperity of Connecticut, it is found in the number of new houses that have been built. You find few of them, very few, in disrepair. Also a number of rural manufacturing plants are being built here on all sides....

But even in this same state much land is for sale. What is the reason? One of the chief ones is the taste for emigration to the West. The desire for improvement embitters the contentment even of the inhabitants of Connecticut. Perhaps this taste comes from the hope of escaping taxes, which, although light and almost nothing in comparison with those of Europe, appear very heavy....

One feels that everything favors the taste for emigration. Newcomers are sure everywhere of finding friends and brothers who speak their own language and admire their courage. They are sure of finding in the country that they reach men who will receive them, aid them. Provisions are cheap the whole way. There is nothing to fear, neither inspectors, nor tolls, nor duties, nor vexations of officers of the police, nor thieves, nor assassins. Here man is as free as the air he breathes. The taste for emigration is daily strengthened by repeated announcements in all the papers of the various emigrant families and of the price of commodities in the western territories. Man everywhere is sheeplike. He says to himself: "Such a one has succeeded; why shall not I succeed! I am nothing here; I shall be something on the Ohio. I work hard here; I shall not work so hard there."...

We passed the night at Fairfield, a town unhappily celebrated in the last war; it suffered all the rage of the English, who burned it. One still sees the vestiges of this infernal fury. Most of the houses are rebuilt; those who have seen the town before the War, miss its ancient state, the air of ease and opulence that distinguished it....

The agreeable part of our journey ended at Fairfield. From there to Rye, 33 miles, we had to struggle against rocks and precipices. I knew not which to admire most in the driver, his bravery or skill. I cannot conceive how he avoided twenty times dashing the carriage to pieces, and how his horses could retain themselves in descending the stairways of rocks. I say stairways and the word is not exaggerated. It is one of these rocks or remarkable precipices that they call Horserock and which offers a chain of rocks so precipitous that if a horse should slip, the carriage would fall two or three hundred feet into a valley.

> The last 31 miles from Rye to New York City were easy, the roads smooth and well graveled. Brissot, with his keen eye for a pretty girl, was charmed by the daughter and mistress of an inn where they stopped for dinner. As they approached New York, he looked with interest at old fortifications that had been used during the Revolution.

Franklin's "Information to Those Who Would Remove to America"

About the time that Benjamin Franklin, in Paris, was helping negotiate the peace treaty that ended the American Revolution, he also wrote an essay explaining to interested Europeans what life in America really was like. Over-optimistic reporters already had written accounts of America that were too glowing. Franklin felt obliged to set the record straight so that only the right kind of immigrants would come to America.

MANY persons in Europe, having by letters, expressed to the writer of this, who is well acquainted with North America, their desire of transporting and establishing themselves in that country; but who appear to him to have formed, through ignorance, mistaken ideas and expectations of what is to be obtained there, he thinks it may be useful, and prevent inconvenient, expensive, and fruitless removals and voyages of improper persons, if he gives some clearer and truer notions of that part of the world than appear to have hitherto prevailed.

He finds it is imagined by numbers that the inhabitants of North America are rich, capable of rewarding, and disposed to reward, all sorts of ingenuity; that they are at the same time ignorant of all the sciences, and, consequently, that strangers, possessing talents in the belles-lettres, fine arts, etc., must be highly esteemed, and so well paid as to become easily rich themselves; that there are also abundance of profitable offices to be disposed of, which the natives are not qualified to fill; and that, having few persons of family among them, strangers of birth must be greatly respected, and of course easily obtain the best of those offices, which will make all their fortunes; that the governments too, to encourage emigration from Europe, not only pay the expense of personal transportation, but give lands gratis to strangers, with Negroes to work for them, utensils of husbandry and stocks of cattle. These are all wild imaginations; and those who go to America with expectations founded upon them will surely find themselves disappointed.

The truth is, that though there are in that country few people so miserable as the poor of Europe, there are also very few that in Europe would be called rich; it is rather a general happy mediocrity that prevails. There are few great proprietors of the soil, and few tenants; most people cultivate their own lands, or follow some handicraft or merchandise; very few rich enough to live idly upon their rents or incomes, or to pay the highest prices given in Europe for painting, statues, architecture, and the other works of art that are more curious than useful.... Of civil offices, or employments, there are few; no superfluous ones, as in Europe; and it is a rule established in some of the states, that no office should be so profitable as to make it desirable....

These ideas prevailing more or less in all the United States, it cannot be worth any man's while, who has a means of living at home, to expatriate himself, in hopes of obtaining a profitable civil office in America; and, as to military offices, they are at an end with the war, the armies being disbanded. Much less is it advisable for a person to go thither, who has no other quality to recommend him but his birth. In Europe it has indeed its value; but it is a commodity that cannot be carried to a worse market than that of America, where people do not inquire concerning a stranger, What is he? but, What can he do? If he has any useful art, he is welcome; and if he exercises it, and behaves well, he will be respected by all that know him; but a mere man of quality, who on that account wants to live upon the public, by some office or salary, will be despised and disregarded. The husbandman is in honor there, and even the mechanic, because their employments are useful. The people have a saying, that God Almighty is Himself a mechanic, the greatest in the universe; and He is respected and admired more for the variety, ingenuity, and utility of His handyworks, than for the antiquity of His family....

With regard to encouragements for strangers from government, they are really only what are derived from good laws and liberty. Strangers are welcome, because there is room enough for them all, and therefore the old inhabitants are not jealous of them; the laws protect them sufficiently, so that they have no need of the patronage of great men; and every one will enjoy securely the profits of his industry. But, if he does not bring a fortune with him, he must work and be industrious to live. One or two years' residence gives him all the rights of a citizen; but the government does not, at present, whatever it may have done in former times, hire people to become settlers, by paying their passages, giving land, Negroes, utensils, stock, or any other kind of emolument whatsoever. In short, America is the land of labour, and by no means what the English call Lubber/and, and the French Pays de Cocagne, where the streets are said to be paved with half-peck loaves, the houses tiled with pancakes, and where the fowls fly about ready roasted, crying, "Come, eat me!"

Who then are the kind of persons to whom an emigration to America may be advantageous? And what are the advantages they may reasonably expect?

Land being cheap in that country, from the vast forests still void of inhabitants, and not likely to be occupied in an age to come, insomuch that the propriety of an hundred acres of fertile soil full of wood may be obtained near the frontiers, in many places, for eight or ten guineas, [A guinea now is worth about $3.00. In purchasing power then, JO guineas was just about the price one would pay for a good horse.] hearty young labouring men, who understand the husbandry of corn and cattle, which is nearly the same in that country as in Europe, may easily establish themselves there. A little money saved of the good wages they receive there, while they work for others, enables them to buy the land and begin their plantation, in which they are assisted by the good will of their neighbors, and some credit. Multitudes of poor people from England, Ireland, Scotland, and Germany have by this means in a few years become wealthy farmers....

From the salubrity of the air, the healthiness of the climate, the plenty of good provisions, and the encouragement to early marriages by the certainty of subsistence in cultivating the earth, the increase of inhabitants by natural generation is very rapid in America, and becomes still more so by the accession of strangers; hence there is a continual demand for more artisans of all the necessary and useful kinds, to supply those cultivators of the earth with houses, and with furniture and utensils of the grosser sorts, which cannot so well be brought from Europe. Tolerably good workmen in any of those mechanic arts are sure to find employ, and to be well paid for their work, there being no restraints preventing strangers from exercising any art they understand, nor any permission necessary. If they are poor, they begin first as servants or journeymen; and if they are sober, industrious, and frugal, they soon become masters, establish themselves in business, marry, raise families, and become respectable citizens.

YELLOW FEVER STRIKES PHILADELPHIA

Life on the farm in the eighteenth century was far healthier than life in town. The minority of Americans who lived in the city existed without modern standards of public health and sanitation.

Before men knew about bacteria and communicable diseases, city dwellers periodically suffered the ravages of plague. The people of Philadelphia were visited by yellow fever again and again in the 1790's. In the following selection, Samuel Breck, a Philadelphia merchant, describes the epidemic which he lived through in 1793. The account is from the Recollections of Samuel Breck, edited by Horace Scudder.

I HAD scarcely become settled in Philadelphia when in July, 1793, the yellow fever broke out, and, spreading rapidly in August, obliged all the citizens who could remove to seek safety in the country. My father took his family to Bristol on the Delaware, and in the last of August I followed him. Having engaged in commerce, and having a ship at the wharf loading for Liverpool, I was compelled to return to the city on the eighth of September and spend the ninth there. My business took me down to the Swedes' church and up Front street to Walnut street wharf, where I had my countinghouse. Everything looked gloomy, and forty-five deaths were reported for the ninth. In the afternoon, when I was about returning to the country, I passed by the lodgings of the Vicomte de Noailles, who had fled from the Revolutionists of France. He was standing at the door, and calling to me, asked me what I was doing in town. "Fly," said he, "as soon as you can, for pestilence is all around us." And yet it was nothing then to what it became three or four weeks later, when from the first to the twelfth of October one thousand persons died. On the twelfth a smart frost came and checked its ravages.

The horrors of this memorable affliction were extensive and heart-rending. Nor were they softened by professional skill. The disorder was in a great measure a stranger to our climate and was awkwardly treated. Its rapid march, being from ten victims a day in August to one hundred a day in October, terrified the physicians, and led them into contradictory modes of treatment. They, as well as the guardians of the city, were taken by surprise. No hospitals or hospital stores were in readiness to alleviate the sufferings of the poor. For a long time nothing could be done other than to furnish coffins for the dead and men to bury them. At length a large house in the neighborhood was appropriately fitted up for the reception of patients, and a few pre-eminent philanthropists volunteered to superintend it. At the head of them was Stephen Girard, who has since become the richest man in America.

In private families the parents, the children, the domestics lingered and died, frequently without assistance. The wealthy soon fled; the fearless or indifferent remained from choice, the poor from necessity. The inhabitants were reduced thus to one-half their number, yet the malignant action of the disease increased, so that those who were in health one day were buried the next. The burning fever occasioned paroxysms of rage which drove the patient naked from his bed to the street, and in some instances to the river, where he was drowned. Insanity was often the last stage of its horrors.

In November, when I returned to the city and found it repeopled, the common topic of conversation could be no other than this unhappy occurrence; the public journals were engrossed by it, and related many examples of calamitous suffering. One of these took place on the property adjacent to my father's. The respectable owner, counting upon the comparative security of his remote residence from the heart of the town, ventured to brave the disorder, and fortunately escaped its attack. He told me that in the height of the sickness, when death was sweeping away its hundreds a week, a man applied to him for leave to sleep one night on the stable floor. The gentleman, like every one else, inspired with fear and caution, hesitated. The stranger pressed his request, assuring him that he had avoided the infected parts of the city, that his health was very good, and promised to go away at sunrise the next day. Under these circumstances he admitted him into his stable for that night. At peep of day the gentleman went to see if the man was gone. On opening the door he found him lying on the floor delirious and in a burning fever.

Fearful of alarming his family, he kept it a secret from them, and went to the committee of health to ask to have the man removed.

That committee was in session day and night at the City Hall in Chestnut street. The spectacle around was new, for he had not ventured for some weeks so low down in town. The attendants on the dead stood on the pavement in considerable numbers soliciting jobs, and until employed they were occupied in feeding their horses out of the coffins which they had provided in anticipation of the daily wants. These speculators were useful, and, albeit with little show of feeling, contributed greatly to lessen, by competition, the charges of interment. The gentleman passed on through these callous spectators until he reached the room in which the committee was assembled, and from whom he obtained the services of a quack doctor, none other being in attendance. They went together to the stable, where the doctor examined the man, and then told the gentleman that at ten o'clock he would send the cart with a suitable coffin, into which he requested to have the dying stranger placed. The poor man was then alive and begging for a drink of water. His fit of delirium had subsided, his reason had returned, yet the experience of the *soi-disant* [*self-styled*] doctor enabled him to foretell that his death would take place in a few hours; it did so, and in time for his corpse to be conveyed away by the cart at the hour appointed. This sudden exit was of common occurrence. The whole number of deaths in 1793 by yellows fever was more than four thousand. Again it took place in 1797, '98 and '99, when the loss was six thousand, making a total in these four years of ten thousand.

II. The Days of Confederation

THE ARTICLES

A long time has passed since Congress has been at the mercy of legislatures in every state. From 1781 (two years before the Peace of Paris officially ended the Revolution) until the Constitution was ratified by nine states in 1788, the United States lived under the loose association provided for by the Articles of Confederation. There were only thirteen of these Articles, and they gave Congress sharply limited powers. The Articles had several crippling defects.

We have printed several of the Articles to show the limitations of authority which made the Confederation unworkable. Note particularly that each state has one vote, regardless of its size or population, that no representative is allowed to serve more than half of the time, and that amendments must be adopted unanimously. The provision in Article VIII for financing the government is one which really helped to doom the Confederation. The Article states that money "shall be supplied by the several states..; that is, Congress could not levy any taxes on its own. This is an interesting document. You can see why it did not work.

Article I: The style of this confederacy shall be "The United States of America."

Article II: Each state retains its sovereignty, freedom, and independence, and every power, jurisdiction, and right, which is not by this confederation expressly delegated to the United States in Congress assembled.

ARTICLE III: The said states hereby severally enter into a firm league of friendship with each other, for their common defense, the security of their liberties, and their mutual and general welfare, binding themselves to assist each other against all force offered to, or attacks made upon them, or any of them, on account of religion, sovereignty, trade, or any other pretense whatever.

ARTICLE V: For the more convenient management of the general interests of the United States, delegates shall be annually appointed in such manner as the legislature of each state shall direct, to meet in Congress on the first Monday in November, in every year, with a power reserved to each state, to recall its delegates, or any of them, at any time within the year, and to send others in their stead, for the remainder of the year.

No state shall be represented in Congress by less than two, nor by more than seven members, and no person shall be capable of being a delegate for more than three years in any term of six years, nor shall any person, being a delegate, be capable of holding any office under the United States, for which he, or another for his benefit receives any salary, fees, or emolument of any kind. Each state shall maintain its own delegates in a meeting of the states, and while they act as members of the committee of the states. In determining questions in the United States, in Congress assembled, each state shall have one vote.

ARTICLE VIII: All charges of war, and all other expenses that shall be incurred for the common defense or general welfare, and allowed by the United States in Congress assembled, shall be defrayed out of a common treasury, which shall be supplied by the several states, in proportion to the value of all land within each state....The taxes for paying that proportion shall be laid and levied by the authority and direction of the legislatures of the several states within the time agreed upon by the United States in Congress assembled.

Article XIII: Every state shall abide by the determinations of the United States in Congress assembled, on all questions which by this confederation are submitted to them. And the articles of this confederation shall be inviolably observed by every state, and the union shall be perpetual; nor shall any alteration at any time hereafter be made in any of them; unless such alteration be agreed to in a Congress of the United States, and be afterwards confirmed by the legislatures of every state.

Many delegates to Congress recognized the weaknesses of the Articles of Confederation. One of them was Jacob Read of South Carolina, who expressed his views on this matter in a letter to George Washington several years before the Constitutional Convention.

Annapolis, 13 August, 1784.

Let the blame fall where it ought—on those, whose attachment to state views, state interests, and state prejudices is so great, as to render them eternally opposed to every measure that can be devised for the public good. The evil is not, however, as yet entirely incurable. I hope and trust the next Congress will be more willing and able to avert the mischiefs that appear to me to threaten the Union. If that cannot be done, we must look about, and see if some more efficient form of government cannot be devised. I have long entertained my doubts of the present form, even if the states were all disposed to be honest, and am sorry to say, such a conclusion would, however, be against premises. I will determine nothing rashly and hope for the best. My most strenuous endeavours shall not be wanting to secure the peace and stability of the Federal Union and the government as long as it is possible; but, I own, I shall not hesitate to join in attempting another when I see from experience that [what] we have instituted is not adequate to the purposes for which it was ordained. Congress either have too little or too much power. To be respectable they must be enabled to enforce an obedience to their ordinances; else why the farce of enacting what no state is bound to execute? If this is denied, Congress is, I think, an unnecessary and useless burden and should not hold from the individual states a great many powers which they cannot exercise and had better be remitted to the individual sovereignties. Of this, more at another time. I ask your Excellency's pardon for so long trespassing on your patience at this time without treating the subject more copiously and conclusively.

SHAYS' REBELLION

Eventually the weaknesses of the Articles of Confederation passed beyond being a subject for debate between those for and those against a strong central government. When Daniel Shays led an uprising of 1,500 angry farmers in western Massachusetts against the authority of the state, the federal government looked on while the state crushed the rebellion. At this point, many responsible men throughout the country saw the United States tottering on the brink of anarchy. One of them was General Washington who, despite his retirement at Mt. Vernon, retained an active interest in public affairs. He wrote his former subordinate, General Benjamin Lincoln, expressing his alarm.

General Lincoln was not sympathetic towards the embattled farmers, but they had genuine grievances. The debt-ridden farmers wanted the state to issue more paper money so that they could pay off their debts and also get relief from the high taxes that the legislature had imposed. The western farmers saw themselves as victims of wealthy property owners and insisted, to the point of rebellion, that they had to have credit to save their farms. The whole episode was perhaps an inevitable after-effect of wartime inflation, but the rebellion showed that a strong federal government was needed. In the two letters that follow, General Lincoln replies to Washington, in the first explaining what he thinks is the real cause of Shays' uprising and in the second describing his successful campaign, at the head of the Massachusetts militia, against Shays.

Hingham, Mass. Dec. 4, 1786

I CANNOT...be surprised to hear your Excellency inquire, "Are your people getting mad? Are we to have the goodly fabric, that eight years were spent in raising, pulled over our heads? What is the cause of all these commotions? When and how will they end?" Although I cannot pretend to give a full and complete answer to them, yet I will make some observations which shall involve in them the best answers to the several questions in my power to give.

"Are your people getting mad?" Many of them appear to be absolutely so, if an attempt to annihilate our present constitution and dissolve the present government can be considered as evidences of insanity.

"Are we to have the goodly fabric, that eight years were spent in rearing, pulled over our heads?" There is great danger that it will be so, I think, unless the tottering system shall be supported by arms, and even then a government which has no other basis than the point of the bayonet, should one be suspended thereon, is so totally· different from the one established, at least in idea, by the different States that if we must have recourse to the sad experiment of arms it can hardly be said that we have supported "the goodly fabric." In this view of the matter, it may be "pulled over our heads." This probably will be the case, for there doth not appear to be virtue enough among the people to preserve a perfect republican government.

"What is the cause of all these commotions?" The causes are too many and too various for me to pretend to trace and point them out. I shall therefore only mention some of those which appear to be the principal ones. Among those I may rank the ease with which property was acquired, with which credit was obtained, and debts were discharged, in the time of the war. Hence people were diverted from their usual industry and economy. A luxuriant mode of living crept into vogue, and soon that income, by which the expenses of all should as much as possible be limited, was no longer considered as having anything to do with the question at what expense families ought to live, or rather which they ought not to have exceeded...

It is impossible for me to determine "when and how they will end"; as I see little probability that they will be brought to a period, and the dignity of government supported, without bloodshed. When a single drop is drawn, the most prophetic spirit will not, in my opinion, be able to determine when it will cease flowing. The proportion of debtors run high in this State. Too many of them are against the government. The men of property and the holders of the public securities are generally supporters of our present constitution. Few of these have been in the field, and it remains quite problematical whether they will in time so fully discover their own interests as they shall be induced thereby to lend for a season part of their property for the security of the remainder. If these classes of men should not turn out on the broad scale with spirit, and the insurgents should take the field and keep it, our constitution will be overturned, and the federal government broken in upon by lopping off one branch essential to the well being of the whole. This cannot be submitted to by the United States with impunity.

February 22, 1787.

THE second of February I was induced to reconnoitre Shays' post on his right, left, and rear. I had received information by General Putnam before, that we could not approach him in front. I intended to have approached him on the third. This reconnoitering gave him an alarm. At 3 o'clock in the morning of the third, I received an application from Wheeler, that he wished to confer with General Putnam. His request was granted. He seemed to have no object but his personal safety. No encouragement being given him on this head, he returned a little after noon; In the evening of the same day, I was informed that Shays had left his ground, and had pointed his route towards Petersham in the County of Worcester, where he intended to make a stand, as a number of towns in the vicinity had engaged to support him.

Our troops were put in motion at eight o'clock. The first part of the night was pleasant, and the weather clement, but between two and three o'clock in the morning, the wind shifting to the westward, it became very cold and squally, with considerable snow. The wind immediately arose very high, and with the light snow which fell the day before and was falling, the paths were soon filled up; the men became fatigued, and they were in a part of the country where they could not be covered in the distance of eight miles, and the cold was so increased, that they could not halt in the road to refresh themselves. Under these circumstances they were obliged to continue their march.

We reached Petersham about nine o'clock in the morning exceedingly fatigued with a march of thirty miles, part of it in a deep snow and in a most violent storm; when this abated, the cold increased and a great proportion of our men were frozen in some part or other, but none dangerously. We approached nearly the centre of the town, where Shays had covered his men; and had we not been prevented from the steepness of a large hill at our entrance, and the depth of the snow, from throwing our men rapidly into it we should have arrested very probably one half this force; for they were so surprised as it was that they had not time to call in their out-parties, or even their guards. About 150 fell into our hands, and none escaped but by the most precipitate flight in different directions.

Thus that body of men who were a few days before offering the grossest insults to the best citizens of this Commonwealth, and were menacing even government itself, were now nearly dispersed, without the shedding of blood but in an instance or two where the insurgents rushed on their own destruction. That so little has been shed is owing in a measure to the patience and obedience, the zeal and the fortitude in our troops, which would have done honor to veterans.

WESTWARD EXPANSION

One of the points of contention between England and America at the time of the Revolution was the matter of westward expansion. In return for Indian help in defeating France, England tried to keep the Ohio Valley intact as a vast Indian preserve. Colonists were forbidden to settle beyond the Appalachian Mountains. Their desire for land, however, was not to be denied, and unauthorized migration took place.

After the Revolution, the illegal trickle of emigration became a lawful flood, and Congress had to provide for developing the land beyond the mountains. Although Kentucky soon became the first western state to join the Union, being admitted on June l, 1792, the entire area north of the Ohio River still was a wilderness. One of the few successes of Congress under the Articles of Confederation was the passage of the Northwest Ordinance in 1787. This bill spelled out the way in which new states would be carved from the huge area; and eventually the Northwest Territory became Ohio, Indiana, Illinois, Wisconsin, and Michigan.

Judge Cooper Plants a Colony

The land beyond the mountains captured the imagination of the Americans, but the Ohio Valley was by no means the only virgin land to be populated after the Revolution. Upstate New York, the beautiful Finger Lake region, also awaited the coming of farmers, and Judge William Cooper, father of the novelist James Fennimore Cooper, played a key role in opening up this area. We like to remember our pioneer ancestors as rugged individualists who hewed the forest and tilled the soil depending only on their strong right arms. This image is only partly true. Judge Cooper's memories, published as A Guide in the Wilderness, make very clear that success on the frontier required capital, able leadership, and cooperation. Here is his account of the founding of Cooperstown:

I*n* 1785 I visited the rough and hilly country of Otsego, where there existed not an inhabitant, nor any trace of a road; I was alone three hundred miles from home, without bread, meat, or food of any kind; fire and fishing tackle were my only means of subsistence. I caught trout in the brook, and roasted them on the ashes. My horse fed on the grass that grew by the edge of the waters. I laid me down to sleep in my watch-coat, nothing but the melancholy wilderness around me. In this way I explored the country, formed my plans of future settlement, and meditated upon the spot where a place of trade or a village should afterwards be established.

In May 1786 I opened the sales of 40,000 acres, which, in sixteen days, were all taken up by the poorest order of men. I soon after established a store, and went to live among them, and continued so to do till 1790, when I brought on my family. For the ensuing four years the scarcity of provisions was a serious calamity; the country was mountainous, there were neither roads nor bridges.

But the greatest discouragement was in the extreme poverty of the people, none of whom had the means of clearing more than a small spot in the midst of the thick and lofty woods, so that their grain grew chiefly in the shade; their maize did not ripen; their wheat was blasted, and the little they did gather they had no mill to grind within twenty miles distance; not one in twenty had a horse, and the way lay through rapid streams, across swamps, or over bogs. They had neither provisions to take with them, nor money to purchase them; nor if they had, were any to be found on their way. If the father of a family went abroad to labour for bread, it cost him three times its value before he could bring it home, and all the business on his farm stood still till his return.

I resided among them, and saw too clearly how bad their condition was. I erected a store-house, and during each winter filled it with large quantities of grain, purchased in distant places. I procured from my friend Henry Drinker a credit for a large quantity of sugar kettles; he also lent me some pot ash kettles, which we conveyed as we best could; sometimes by partial roads on sleighs, and sometimes over the ice. By this means I established pot ash works among the settlers, and made them debtor for their bread and labouring utensils. I also gave them credit for their maple sugar and pot ash, at a price that would bear transportation, and the first year after the adoption of this plan I collected in one mass forty-three hogsheads of sugar, and three hundred barrels of pot and pearl ash, worth about nine thousand dollars. This kept the people together and at home, and the country soon assumed a new face.

I had not funds of my own sufficient for the opening of new roads, but I collected the people at convenient seasons, and by joint efforts we were able to throw bridges over the deep streams, and to make... such roads as suited our then humble purposes.

In the winter preceding the summer of 1789, grain rose in Albany to a price before unknown. The demand swept the whole granaries of the Mohawk country. The number of beginners who depended upon it for their bread greatly aggravated the evil, and a famine ensued, which will never be forgotten by those who, though now in the enjoyment of ease and comfort, were then afflicted with the cruelest of wants.

In the month of April I arrived amongst them with several loads of provisions, destined for my own use and that of the labourers I had brought with me for certain necessary operations; but in a few days all was gone, and there remained not one pound of salt meat nor a single biscuit. Many were reduced to such distress, as to live upon the roots of wild leeks; some more fortunate lived upon milk, whilst others supported nature by drinking a syrup made of maple sugar and water. The quantity of leeks they ate had such an effect upon their breath, that they could be smelled at many paces distance, and when they came together, it was like cattle that had pastured in a garlic field. A man of the name of Beets, mistaking some poisonous herb for a leek, ate it, and died in consequence. Judge of my feelings at this epoch, with two hundred families about me, and not a morsel of bread.

A singular event seemed sent by a good Providence to our relief; it was reported to me that unusual shoals of fish were seen moving in the clear waters of the Susquehanna. I went and was surprised to find that they were herrings. We made something like a small net, by the interweaving of twigs, and by this rude and simple contrivance, we were able to take them in thousands. In less than ten days each family had an ample supply with plenty of salt. I also obtained from the Legislature, then in session, seventeen hundred bushels of corn. This we packed on horses' backs, and on our arrival made a distribution among the families, in proportion to the number of individuals of which each was composed.

This was the first settlement I made, and the first attempted after the Revolution; it was, of course, attended with the greatest difficulties; nevertheless, to its success many others have owed their origin.... When I contemplate all this, and above all, when I see these good old settlers meet together, and hear them talk of past hardships, of which I bore my share, and compare the misery they then endured with the comforts they now enjoy, my emotions border upon weakness, which manhood can scarcely avow.

The Founding of Marietta, Ohio

On March 1, 1786, a group of ex-Revolutionary army officers gathered at the Bunch of Grapes Tavern in Boston. Their purpose was to set up an organization to sell land in the Northwest Territory. The result of their meeting was the Ohio Company, which negotiated a contract with Congress to develop one and one-half million acres of land in southeastern Ohio. These energetic New Englanders succeeded in surveying their tract and settling farmers on it. Within two years they founded the town of Marietta. By 1803, Ohio had grown populous enough to become the seventeenth state in the Union.

Colonel John May, one of the ex-soldiers who invested in Ohio land, left Boston to live in the new town. From his diary we have extracted scattered entries for the year 1788. He gives us an intimate glimpse of day-to-day life during the settling of the new town.

MAY 12th, 1788, Monday. I am still in quarters opposite Pittsburgh, living as cheaply as if I was at Muskingum. Am waiting for the boat to carry us all down.... Yesterday two boats for Kentucky hauled in at our landing, having on board twenty-nine whites, twenty-four Negroes, nine dogs, twenty-three horses, cows, hogs, etc., besides provision and furniture. Several have passed today equally large....

Wednesday, 21st. At 2 o'clock P.M. our boat—oh, be joyful!—hove in sight, coming around the point, and, in half an hour, was made fast at Pittsburgh. She is forty-two feet long and twelve feet wide, with cover. She will carry a burden of forty-five tons, and draws only two and one half feet water....

Saturday, 24th. At 12 ½ o'clock cast off our fasts, and committed ourselves to the current of the Ohio. The scene was beautiful. Without wind or waves, we, insensibly almost, make more than five miles an hour....

Monday, 26th. Thus we moved on, constantly espying new wonders and beauties, till 3 o'clock, when we arrived safely on the banks of the delightful Muskingum.

Tuesday, 27th. Slept on board last night, and rose early this morning. Have spent the day in reconnoitering the spot where the city is to be laid out, and find it to answer the best descriptions I have ever heard of it. The situation delightfully agreeable, and well calculated for an elegant city....

As to our surveying, buildings, etc., they are in a very backward way. Little appears to be done, and a great deal of time and money misspent....

Thursday, 29th. This day the axe is laid to the root of the trees. In order to do this my people were armed with the suitable tool, and went forth to smite the ancient tenants of the woods. Venison plenty at 1 pence or one copper per pound. I was engaged all the afternoon with the surveyors. Find the soil very good, but was tormented beyond measure by myriads of gnats. They not only bite surprisingly, but get down one's throat.

This evening, arrived two long boats from the Rapids, with officers and soldiers, the number about one hundred. On their passage up the river they were fired upon by a strong party of Indians, headed by a white man. They returned the fire, and had two men killed. They were obliged to drop down the river a piece, and come by the place in the night....

Saturday, 31st. All hands at work on my ten-acre lot. Took hold of it with spirit. There are six of us in all, and we completely cleared an acre and a half by sunset. The land as good as any that can be found in the universe....

Tuesday, June 10th....The people hewing timber for the house, which I am in hopes to raise in eight or ten days; for I am not very comfortable on board my Kentucky ship. Met this morning, according to adjournment, and after much debate and discussion, agreed to cut up our commons into three-acre lots, to be drawn for in July. This has appeased the minds of the people. We also appointed officers of police.

Wednesday, 11th. I have enlarged my gang today, which I have divided into three squads: four men hewing timber; two clearing land; and two digging a cellar in the bank, near my boat. This conveniency is much wanted to keep the beer and other matters in. We have dug no wells as yet, and the river water is too warm to be pleasant....

Sunday, 15th. A number of poor devils—five in all—took their departure homeward this morning. They came from home moneyless and brainless, and have returned as they came....

Tuesday, 17th. This evening Judge Parsons' and General Varnum's commissions were read; also, regulations for the government of the people. In fact, by-laws were much wanted. Officers were named to command the militia; guards to be mounted every evening; all males more than fifteen years old to appear under arms every Sunday....

Friday, July 4th. All labor comes to a pause today in memory of the Declaration of Independence. Our long bowery is built on the east bank of the Muskingum; a table laid sixty feet long, in plain sight of the garrison, at one-quarter of a mile distance. At 1 o'clock General Harmer and his lady, Mrs. McCurders, and all the officers not on duty came over, and several other gentlemen. An excellent oration was delivered by Judge Varnum, and the cannon fired a salute of fourteen guns....

Friday, 11th. A delightful day. All hands at work on the house. This an arduous undertaking, and will cost more than I intended. Am building from several motives. First, for the benefit of the settlement; second, from a prospect or hope of gain hereafter; third, for an asylum for myself and family, should we ever want it; fourth, as a place where I can leave my stores and baggage in safety; and lastly, to gratify a foolish ambition, I suppose it is. The house is thirty-six feet long, eighteen wide, and fifteen high; a good cellar under it, and drain; and is the first (of the kind) built in Marietta....

Monday, 14th. All hands at work on the house. Eat green peas today from my own garden, planted exactly five weeks ago. All this trusting to Providence but a little while. Things do grow amazingly!

FOREIGN AFFAIRS

Domestic affairs held the center of the stage in the days of the Articles of Confederation, but the young republic at the same time was taking its place in the community of nations. John Adams was the first American minister to England. You can imagine the feelings of Adams as he presented his credentials to King

George III, whose sovereignty he had rebelled against less than ten years before.

He wanted to present his credentials as quietly as possible and then disappear, but the foreign secretary, Lord Carmarthen, said he would be expected to make a speech. He did so forthrightly, as he did everything, and in the selection that follows we find him waiting anxiously in the antechamber of the king's audience room. His report comes from a letter he wrote on June 2, 1785, to John Jay, who was then Secretary for Foreign Affairs.

WHILE I stood in this place, where it seems all ministers stand upon such occasions, always attended by the master of ceremonies, the room very full of ministers of state, lords, and bishops, and all sorts of courtiers, as well as the next room which is the King's bedchamber, you may well suppose I was the focus of all eyes. I was relieved, however, from the embarrassment of it by the Swedish and Dutch ministers, who came to me, and entertained me in a very agreeable conversation during the whole time. Some other gentlemen, whom I had seen before, came to make their compliments too, until the Marquis of Carmarthen returned and desired me to go with him to his Majesty. I went with his Lordship through the levee room into the King's closet. The door was shut, and I was left with his Majesty and the secretary of state alone. I made the three reverences,—one at the door, another about half way, and a third before the presence,—according to the usage established at this and all the northern Courts of Europe, and then addressed myself to his Majesty in the following words:—

"Sir,—The United States of America have appointed me their minister plenipotentiary to your Majesty, and have directed me to deliver to your Majesty this letter which contains the evidence of it. It is in obedience to their express commands, that I have the honor to assure your Majesty of their unanimous disposition and desire to cultivate the most friendly and liberal intercourse between your

Majesty's subjects and their citizens, and of their best wishes for your Majesty's health and happiness, and for that of your royal family. The appointment of a minister from the United States to your Majesty's Court will form an epoch in the history of England and of America.

"I think myself more fortunate than all my fellow-citizens, in having the distinguished honor to be the first to stand in your Majesty's royal presence in a diplomatic character; and I shall esteem myself the happiest of men, if 1 can be instrumental in recommending my country more and more to your Majesty's royal benevolence, and of restoring an entire esteem, confidence, and affection, or, in better words, the old good nature and the old good humor between people, who, though separated by an ocean, and under different governments, have the same language, a similar religion, and kindred blood."...

The King listened to every word I said, with dignity, but with an apparent emotion. Whether it was the nature of the interview, or whether it was my visible agitation, for I felt more than I did or could express, that touched him, I cannot say. But he was much affected, and answered me with more tremor than I had spoken with, and said:—

"Sir,—The circumstances of this audience are so extraordinary, the language you have now held is so extremely proper, and the feelings you have discovered so justly adapted to the occasion, that I must say that I not only receive with pleasure the assurance of the friendly dispositions of the United States, but that I am very glad the choice has fallen upon you to be their minister. I wish you, sir, to believe, and that it may be understood in America, that I have done nothing in the late contest but what I thought myself indispensably bound to do, by the duty which I owed to my people. I will be very frank with you. I was the last to consent to the separation; but the separation having been made, and having become inevitable, I have always said, as I say now, that I would be the first to meet the friendship of the United States as an independent power. The moment I see such sentiments and language as yours prevail, and a disposition to give to this country the preference, that moment I shall say, let the circumstances of language, religion, and blood have their natural and full effect."

I dare not say that these were the King's precise words, and, it is even possible, that I may have in some particular mistaken his meaning;...This I do say, that the foregoing is his Majesty's meaning as I then understood it, and his own words as nearly as I can recollect them.

III. The Constitution

THE CONVENTION AT WORK

As we have seen, the weakness of the Articles of Confederation created a need for a stronger government. For this reason delegates from five states met in Annapolis in 1786 to consider strengthening the Articles, but they could not accomplish anything important because they represented only a minority of states. They did pass a resolution proposed by Alexander Hamilton calling for another convention the next year, and in May, 1787, the Constitutional Convention began its work in Philadelphia.

An excellent case could be made to show that the summer of 1787 was the most crucial period in the history of the United States. The signing of the Declaration of Independence was, indeed, a historic and dramatic moment; so was the surrender of Lord Cornwallis at Yorktown. In contrast, the Constitutional Convention did its work with no fanfare of publicity, and the debate plodded on day after day from May to September behind closed doors. Yet the result was far-reaching: the Convention drafted the basic law under which we still live. Without the work of the Convention there might be no United States today.

We are fortunate that James Madison kept a detailed journal of the Convention. In it he reported all the resolutions, votes, and speeches so that we can follow the work of the delegates as though we were present. We know more than the Convention's contemporaries did, because Madison's journal was not published until after his death in 1836. The framers of the Constitution did not want the public to be swayed by the frank objections raised at the Convention to articles later agreed upon. They wanted only the finished product submitted to ratifying conventions in the various states.

The Convention opened with the presentation of Virginia's plan for a Constitution. This plan, with modifications, is substantially the organizational pattern finally adopted by the delegates after lengthy deliberations. Basically, it called for division of the government into the familiar three branches—legislative, executive, and judicial. The legislative branch was to be composed of two houses.

The first decision that had to be made was how to elect representatives. You may be surprised to learn that not all members of the Convention trusted the people to elect their own Congressmen. The Mr. Randolph referred to is Edmund Randolph, who presented the Virginia Plan. The speakers are Roger Sherman of Connecticut, Elbridge Gerry of Massachusetts, George Mason of Virginia, James Wilson of Pennsylvania, Pierce Butler of South Carolina, and James Madison:

In Committee of the whole on Mr. Randolph's propositions.

The third resolution "that the national legislature ought to consist of two branches" was agreed to without debate or dissent, except that of Pennsylvania, given probably from complaisance to Dr. Franklin who was understood to be partial to a single house of legislation.

Resolution 4, first clause, "that the members of the first branch of the national legislature ought to be elected by the people of the several states," being taken up,

Mr. Sherman opposed the election by the people, insisting that it ought to be by the state legislatures. The people, he said, immediately should have as little to do as may be about the government.

They want [Lack] information and are constantly liable to be misled.

Mr. Gerry. The evils we experience flow from the excess of democracy. The people do not want virtue, but are the dupes of pretended patriots. In Massachusetts it had been fully confirmed by experience that they are daily misled into the most baneful measures and opinions by the false reports circulated by designing men, and which no one on the spot can refute. One principal evil arises from the want of due provision for those employed in the administration of government. It would seem to be a maxim of democracy to starve the public servants. He mentioned the popular clamour in Massachusetts for the reduction of salaries and the attack made on that of the governor though secured by the spirit of the constitution itself. He had, he said, been too republican heretofore: he was still, however, republican, but had been taught by experience the danger of the levelling spirit.

Mr. Mason argued strongly for an election of the larger branch by the people. It was to be the grand depository of the democratic principle of the government. It was, so to speak, to be our House of Commons—It ought to know and sympathize with every part of the community; and ought therefore to be taken not only from different parts of the whole republic, but also from different districts of the larger members of it, which had in several instances, particularly in Virginia, different interests and views arising from difference of produce, of habits, etc.

He admitted that we had been too democratic but was afraid we should incautiously run into the opposite extreme. We ought to attend to the rights of every class of the people. He had often wondered at the indifference of the superior classes of society to this dictate of humanity and policy, considering that however affluent their circumstances, or elevated their situations might be, the course of a few years, not only might but certainly would, distribute their posterity throughout the lowest classes of society. Every selfish motive therefore, every family attachment, ought to recommend such a system of policy as would provide no less carefully for the rights and happiness of the lowest than of the highest orders of citizens.

Mr. Wilson contended strenuously for drawing the most numerous branch of the legislature immediately from the people. He was for raising the federal pyramid to a considerable altitude, and for that reason wished to give it as broad a basis as possible. No government could long subsist without the confidence of the people. In a republican government this confidence was peculiarly essential. He also thought it wrong to increase the weight of the state legislatures by making them the electors of the national legislature. All interference between the general and local government should be obviated as much as possible. On examination it would be found that the opposition of states to federal measures had proceeded much more from the officers of the states, than from the people at large.

Mr. Madison considered the popular election of one branch of the national legislature as essential to every plan of free government. He observed that in some of the states one branch of the legislature was composed of men already removed from the people by an intervening body of electors; that if the first branch of the general legislature should be elected by the state legislatures, the second branch elected by the first—the executive by the second together with the first; and other appointments again made for subordinate purposes by the executive, the people would be lost sight of altogether; and the necessary sympathy between them and their rulers and officers, too little felt....

Mr. Gerry did not like the election by the people. The maxims taken from the British Constitution were often fallacious when applied to our situation which was extremely different. Experience he said had shown that the state legislatures drawn immediately from the people did not always possess their confidence. He had no objection however to an election by the people if it were so qualified that men of honor and character might not be unwilling to be joined in the appointments. He seemed to think the people might nominate a certain number out of which the state legislatures should be bound to choose.

Mr. Butler thought an election by the people an impracticable mode.

On the question for an election of the first branch of the national legislature, by the people,

Massachusetts, aye. Connecticut, divided. New York, aye. New Jersey, no. Pennsylvania, aye. Delaware, divided. Virginia, aye. North Carolina, aye. South Carolina, no. Georgia, aye.

On June 15th, William Paterson of New Jersey laid before the Convention another plan, representing the desires of the small states. His plan called for amending the Articles of Confederation, not the writing of an entire new constitution. He argued that the Convention did not have authority to do more than revise the Articles, but his real purpose was to preserve the voting procedures of the Confederation that gave each state an equal vote.

MR. PATERSON said, as he had on a former occasion given his sentiments on the plan proposed by Mr. Randolph, he would now, avoiding repetition as much as possible, give his reasons in favor of that proposed by himself. He preferred it because it accorded 1, with the powers of the Convention; 2, with the sentiments of the people. If the confederacy was radically wrong, let us return to our states, and obtain larger powers, not assume them ourselves. I came here not to speak my own sentiments, but the sentiments of those who sent me. Our object is not such a government as may be best in itself, but such a one as our constituents have authorized us to prepare, and as they will approve.

If we argue the matter on the supposition that no Confederacy at present exists, it can not be denied that all the states stand on the footing of equal sovereignty. All therefore must concur before any can be bound. If a proportional representation be right, why do we not vote so here? If we argue on the fact that a federal compact actually exists, and consult the articles of it, we still find an equal sovereignty to be the basis of it. He reads the fifth article of Confederation giving each State a vote—and the thirteenth declaring that no alteration shall be made without unanimous consent. This is the nature of all treaties. What is unanimously done, must be unanimously undone....

Mr. Randolph was not scrupulous on the point of power. When the salvation of the Republic was at stake, it would be treason to our trust, not to propose what we found necessary. He painted in strong colours, the imbecility of the existing Confederacy, and the danger of delaying a substantial reform.

> Alexander Hamilton, who was to play an important role in government after the Convention, took relatively little part in the debate. He made his only speech on June 18th. In it he candidly declared that neither the Virginia nor the New Jersey plan satisfied him. He favored a British-type constitutional monarchy. In the selection that follows Madison reports part of Hamilton's address.

In his private opinion he had no scruple in declaring, supported as he was by the opinion of so many of the wise and good, that the British government was the best in the world: and that he doubted much whether anything short of it would do in America. He hoped gentlemen of different opinions would bear with him in this, and begged them to recollect the change of opinion on this subject which had taken place and was still going on....

In every community where industry is encouraged, there will be a division of it into the few and the many. Hence separate interests will arise. There will be debtors and creditors, etc. Give all power to the many, they will oppress the few. Give all power to the few, they will oppress the many. Both therefore ought to have the power, that each may defend itself against the other. To the want of this check we owe our paper money, instalment laws, etc. To the proper adjustment of it the British owe the excellence of their constitution.

Their house of Lords is a most noble institution. Having nothing to hope for by a change, and a sufficient interest by means of their property, in being faithful to the national interest, they form a permanent barrier against every pernicious innovation, whether attempted on the part of the Crown or of the Commons. No temporary Senate will have firmness enough to answer the purpose.... As to the Executive, it seemed to be admitted that no good one could be established on Republican principles. Was not this giving up the merits of the question; for can there be a good government without a good Executive. The· English model was the only good one on this subject. The hereditary interest of the King was so interwoven with that of the nation, and his personal emoluments so great, that he was placed above the danger of being corrupted from abroad—and at the same time was both sufficiently independent and sufficiently controlled, to answer the purpose of the institution at home.

In due time the Convention agreed to elect the House of Representatives by direct vote of the people according to population. This meant that the large states would have more members in the House than the small states, just as they still do. In addition, the large states also wanted to elect the Senate according to population. Both groups already had decided that the Senate was to be elected by the state legislatures, because they did not trust the public enough to let it elect the entire Congress. The small states, however, would not give ground on the representation of the Senate, and they carried their point. The following debate on this matter has been taken from Madison's journal for July 7.

"Shall the clause allowing each State one vote in the second branch, stand as part of the report?" being taken up—

Mr. Gerry. This is the critical question. He had rather agree to it than have no accommodation. A government short of a proper national plan, if generally acceptable, would be preferable to a proper one which if it could be carried at all, would operate on discontented states. He thought it would be best to suspend the question till the committee yesterday appointed should make report.

Mr. Sherman supposed that it was the wish of every one that some general government should be established. An equal vote in the second branch would, he thought, be most likely to give it the necessary vigor. The small states have more vigor in their governments than the large ones; the more influence therefore the large ones have, the weaker will be the government. In the large states it will be most difficult to collect the real and fair sense of the people. Fallacy and undue influence will be practised with most success; and improper men will most easily get into office. If they vote by states in the second branch, and each state has an equal vote, there must be always a majority of states as well as a majority of the people on the side of public measures, and the government will have decision and efficacy. If this be not the case in the second branch there may be a majority of states against public measures, and the difficulty of compelling them to abide by the public determination, will render the government feebler than it has ever yet been....

On question shall the words stand as part of the report?

Massachusetts, divided. Connecticut, aye. New York, aye. New Jersey, aye. Pennsylvania, no. Delaware, aye. Maryland, aye. Virginia, no. North Carolina, aye. South Carolina, no. Georgia, divided.

SIGNING THE CONSTITUTION

The Convention came to a dramatic conclusion on September 17th, 1787, when the work was finished and the delegates gathered to sign the historic document. At that moment Benjamin Franklin rose with a speech in his hand. Aside from George Washington, who had been elected president of the Convention, Franklin was the most distinguished member of the group. He was then 81 years old, in the twilight of his distinguished career. Being too feeble to deliver his own speech, he handed it to James Wilson, who read as follows:

Mr. President:

I CONFESS that there are several parts of this constitution which I do not at present approve, but I am not sure I shall never approve them: for having lived long, I have experienced many instances of being obliged by better information or fuller consideration, to change opinions even on important subjects, which I once thought right, but found to be otherwise. It is therefore that the older I grow, the more apt I am to doubt my own judgment, and to pay more respect to the judgment of others.

Most men indeed, as well as most sects in religion, think themselves in possession of all truth, and that wherever others differ from them it is so far error.

In these sentiments, Sir, I agree to this Constitution with all its faults, if they are such; because I think a general government necessary for us, and there is no form of government but what may be a blessing to the people if well administered, and believe farther that this is likely to be well administered for a course of years, and can only end in despotism, as other forms have done before it, when the people shall become so corrupted as to need despotic government, being incapable of any other.

I doubt too whether any other convention we can obtain may be able to make a better constitution. For when you assemble a number of men to have the advantage of their joint wisdom, you inevitably assemble with those men, all their prejudices, their passions, their errors of opinion, their local interests, and their selfish views. From such an assembly can a perfect production be expected? It therefore astonishes me, Sir, to find this system approaching so near to perfection as it does; and I think it will astonish our enemies, who are waiting with confidence to hear that our councils are confounded like those of the builders of Babel; and that our states are on the point of separation, only to meet hereafter for the purpose of cutting one another's throats.

Thus I consent, Sir, to this constitution because I expect no better, and because I am not sure, that it is not the best. The opinions I have had of its errors, I sacrifice to the public good....

Much of the strength and efficiency of any government in procuring and securing happiness to the people, depends on opinion, on the general opinion of the goodness of the government, as well as of the wisdom and integrity of its governors. I hope therefore that for our own sakes as a part of the people, and for the sake of posterity, we shall act heartily and unanimously in recommending this constitution (if approved by Congress and confirmed by the conventions) wherever our influence may extend, and turn our future thoughts and endeavors to the means of having it well administered.

On the whole, Sir, I cannot help expressing a wish that every member of the convention who may still have objections to it, would with me, on this occasion doubt a little of his own infallibility, and to make manifest our unanimity, put his name to this instrument.

Soon after the delegates had heard Franklin's speech, all but three, Randolph, Mason, and Gerry, signed the document, and the chairman, George Washington, adjourned the Convention. The next task was to persuade the states to ratify the Constitution. But before adjournment, as the last signers were writing their names, Franklin looked towards the president's chair, behind which was painted a rising sun. He remarked to delegates near him that painters had found it difficult to distinguish in their art a rising from a setting sun: "I have," said he, "often and often in the course of the session...looked at that behind the President without being able to tell whether it was rising or setting, but now at length I have the happiness to know that it is a rising and not a setting sun."

RATIFYING THE CONSTITUTION

Between September and the next June a public debate over the Constitution went on from New England to Georgia. By the summer of 1788 the necessary nine states had ratified, and the Constitution was put into effect. The most influential factor in persuading people to accept the Constitution was a series of newspaper articles written by Madison, Hamilton, and Jay. This series, known today as The Federalist, has become a classic among American books. Even now no one has surpassed its convincing arguments in support of the American Constitution. In the selection that follows we have used part of Number Two of The Federalist. John Jay, who became the first Chief Justice of the Supreme Court, is its author.

To the People of the State of New York:

When the people of America reflect that they are now called upon to decide a question, which, in its consequences, must prove one of the most important that ever engaged their attention, the propriety of their taking a very comprehensive, as well as a very serious, view of it, will be evident.

Nothing is more certain than the indispensable necessity of government, and it is equally undeniable, that whenever and however it is instituted, the people must cede to it some of their natural rights, in order to vest it with requisite powers. It is well worthy of consideration, therefore, whether it would conduce more to the interest of the people of America that they should, to all general purposes, be one nation, under one federal government, or that they should divide themselves into separate confederacies, and give to the head of each the same kind of powers which they are advised to place in one national government.

It has until lately been a received and uncontradicted opinion, that the prosperity of the people of America depended on their continuing firmly united, and the wishes, prayers, and efforts of our best and wisest citizens have been constantly directed to that object. But politicians now appear, who insist that this opinion is erroneous, and that instead of looking for safety and happiness in union, we ought to seek it in a division of the States into distinct confederacies or sovereignties....

This country and this people seem to have been made for each other, and it appears as if it was the design of Providence, that an inheritance so proper and convenient for a band of brethren, united to each other by the strongest ties, should never be split into a number of unsocial, jealous, and alien sovereignties.

Similar sentiments have hitherto prevailed among all orders and denominations of men among us. To all general purposes we have uniformly been one people; each individual citizen everywhere enjoying the same national rights, privileges, and protection. As a nation we have made peace and war; as a nation we have vanquished our common enemies; as a nation we have formed alliances, and made treaties, and entered into various compacts and conventions with foreign states.

A strong sense of the value and blessings of union induced the people, at a very early period, to institute a federal government to preserve and perpetuate it. They formed it almost as soon as they had a political existence; nay, at a time when their habitations were in flames, when many of their citizens were bleeding, and when the progress of hostility and desolation left little room for those calm and mature inquiries and reflections which must ever precede the formation of a wise and well-balanced government for a free people. It is not to be wondered at, that a government instituted in times so inauspicious, should on experiment be found greatly deficient...to the purpose it was intended to answer.

This intelligent people perceived and regretted these defects. Still continuing no less attached to union than enamoured of liberty, they observed the danger which immediately threatened the former and more remotely the latter; and being persuaded that ample security for both could only be found in a national government more wisely framed, they, as with one voice, convened the late convention at Philadelphia, to take that important subject under consideration.

This convention, composed of men who possessed the confidence of the people, and many of whom had become highly distinguished by their patriotism, virtue, and wisdom, in times which tried the minds and hearts of men, undertook the arduous task. In the mild season of peace, with minds unoccupied by other subjects, they passed many months in cool, uninterrupted, and daily consultation; and finally, without having been awed by power, or influenced by any passions except love for their country, they presented and recommended to the people the plan produced by their joint and very unanimous councils.

IV. Washington's Administration

JEFFERSON'S VIEWS OF HAMILTON AND THE ADMINISTRATION

Despite their wisdom, the members of the Constitutional Convention did not anticipate the growth of American political parties. But as soon as the Constitution was submitted to the states for ratification, differences of opinion began to arise over the role of the new government in the nation's life. Some believed that the best government was the one that governed least; others thought that the federal government should assume all powers not specifically given to the states.

During Washington's administration these differences began to be sharply defined. The President, perhaps unwittingly, contributed to the rise of parties by appointing to his Cabinet the two leading spokesmen for the opposing points of view. Thomas Jefferson was called home from his post as American minister to France to become Secretary of State. Alexander Hamilton was named Secretary of the Treasury. These two men challenged each other at every turn on issues both domestic and foreign.

The following selection comes from the notes that Jefferson wrote late in his life for a continuation of his autobiography. He gives a vivid picture of life in New York in Washington's administration and a glimpse of the role Hamilton played in the Cabinet.

> Keep in mind that while Jefferson thought Hamilton an honorable man in private life, he deplored his political principles.

I RETURNED from that mission in the first year of the new government, having landed in Virginia in December, 1789, and proceeded to New York in March, 1790, to enter on the office of Secretary of State. Here, certainly, I found a state of things which, of all I had ever contemplated, I the least expected. I had left France in the first year of its revolution, in the fervor of natural rights, and zeal for reformation. My conscientious devotion to these rights could not be heightened, but it had been aroused and excited by daily exercise. The President received me cordially, and my colleagues and the circle of principal citizens, apparently, with welcome. The courtesies of dinner parties given me, as a stranger newly arrived among them, placed me at once in their familiar society. But I cannot describe the wonder and mortification with which the table conversations filled me. Politics were the chief topic, and a preference of kingly over republican government was evidently the favorite sentiment. An apostate I could not be, nor yet a hypocrite; and I found myself, for the most part, the only advocate on the republican side of the question, unless among the guests there chanced to be some member of that party from the legislative Houses.

Hamilton's financial system had then passed. It had two objects: first, as a puzzle, to exclude popular understanding and inquiry; second, as a machine for the corruption of the legislature; for he avowed the opinion that man could be governed by one of two motives only, force or interest; force, he observed, in this country was out of the question, and the interests, therefore, of the members must be laid hold of, to keep the legislative in unison with the executive. And with grief and shame it must be acknowledged that his machine was not without effect....

But Hamilton was not only a monarchist, but for a monarchy bottomed on corruption. In proof of this, I will relate an anecdote, for the truth of which I attest the God who made me. Before the President set out on his southern tour in April, 1791, he addressed a letter of the fourth of that month, from Mount Vernon, to the Secretaries of State, Treasury and War, desiring that if any serious and important cases should arise during his absence, they would consult and act on them. And he requested that the Vice President should also be consulted. This was the only occasion on which that officer was ever requested to take part in a cabinet question. Some occasion for consultation arising, I invited those gentlemen (and the Attorney General, as well as I remember) to dine with me, in order to confer on the subject. After the cloth was removed, and our question agreed and dismissed, conversation began on other matters, and by some circumstance, was led to the British constitution, on which Mr. Adams observed, "Purge that constitution of its corruption, and give to its popular branch equality of representation, and it would be the most perfect constitution ever devised by the wit of man." Hamilton paused and said, "Purge it of its corruption, and give to its popular branch equality of representation, and it would become an impracticable government: as it stands at present, with all its supposed defects, it is the most perfect government which ever existed." And this was assuredly the exact line which separated the political creeds of these two gentlemen. The one was for two hereditary branches and an honest elective one; the other, for an hereditary King, with a House of Lords and Commons corrupted to his will, and standing between him and the people.

Hamilton was, indeed, a singular character. Of acute understanding, disinterested, honest, and honorable in all private transactions, amiable in society, and duly valuing virtue in private life, yet so bewitched and perverted by the British example, as to be under thorough conviction that corruption was essential to the government of a nation.

HAMILTON'S VIEW OF JEFFERSON

We now give Hamilton a chance to have his say about Jefferson. The reference to the funding system is to the plan which Hamilton was instrumental in obtaining whereby the federal government took over debts incurred by the states before the United States came into existence. Hamilton supported this measure in order to make the government strong, to force creditors to look to one national government, rather than thirteen state governments, for payment. Jefferson opposed the measure because speculators who had bought up nearly worthless state notes of indebtedness would profit enormously. This selection is from a letter Hamilton wrote to an old friend, Colonel Carrington of Virginia.

Philadelphia, May 26, 1792

IT was not, till the last session, that I became unequivocally convinced of the following truth: "that Mr. Madison, co-operating with Mr. Jefferson, is at the head of a faction, decidedly hostile to me, and my administration; and actuated by views, in my judgment, subversive of the principles of good government, and dangerous to the Union, peace and happiness of the country....

This conviction, in my mind, is the result of a long train of circumstances, many of them minute. To attempt to detail them all would fill a volume. I shall therefore confine myself to the mention of a few.

First, as to the point of opposition to me, and my administration.

Mr. Jefferson, with very little reserve, manifests his dislike of the funding system, generally, calling in question the expediency of funding a debt at all. Some expressions, which he has dropped in my own presence, (sometimes without sufficient attention to delicacy), will not permit me to doubt on this point representations which I have had from various respectable quarters. I do not mean that he advocates directly the undoing of what has been done; but he censures the whole, on principles, which, if they should become general, could not but end in the subversion of the system.

In various conversations, with foreigners as well as citizens, he has thrown censure on my principles of government and on my measures of administration. He has predicted that the people would not long tolerate my proceedings and that I should not long maintain my ground. Some of those whom he immediately and notoriously moves, have even whispered suspicions of the rectitude of my motives and conduct. In the question concerning the Bank he not only delivered an opinion in writing against its constitutionality and expediency, but he did it in a style and manner which I felt as partaking of asperity and ill humor towards me. As one of the trustees of the sinking fund, I have experienced in almost every leading question opposition from him. When any turn of things in the community has threatened either odium or embarrassment to me, he has not been able to suppress the satisfaction which it gave him.

THE JAY TREATY

The new Constitution had barely been put into effect when the French Revolution began. The political and economic upheavals of that revolution convulsed Europe and brought the United States to her first crisis. England, trying to keep the French Revolution from spreading, went to war with France in 1795, and in order to shut off French trade, British captains were ordered to seize ships carrying cargoes to France. The result was that hundreds of American vessels were captured.

Meantime, the British never had abandoned their forts on the northwest frontier, and their Indian allies continued to harass settlers in the Ohio Valley. By 1794 the United States was close to war with Great Britain. War, however, would have wrecked the young republic. At this point, President Washington sent Chief Justice John Jay to England to negotiate a treaty to obtain redress for England's interference with our shipping and her refusal to remove her troops from our frontiers. Jay returned in 1795 with a treaty—the best he could get—but it was not good enough to satisfy the Anti-Federalists.

Jay was denounced by Jefferson's followers, and the debate in Congress over the treaty was bitter. The treaty did promise that the British would evacuate the northwest forts and settle claims for seized shipping. But England did not agree to stop impressing American seamen into the British navy or to stop capturing American ships carrying goods to France. Nevertheless, the treaty did prevent war with England and insured this country's survival. It also set up commissions to settle outstanding disputes, an innovation of Jay's which was to be followed in the peaceful settlement of later differences between Great Britain and the United States.

The next selection is part of a speech delivered in Congress on April 28, 1796, in support of the treaty by Fisher Ames, a leading Federalist.

THE treaty is bad, fatally bad, is the cry. It sacrifices the interest, the honor, the independence of the United States, and the faith of our engagements to France. If we listen to the clamor of party intemperance, the evils of it are of a number not to be counted, and of a nature not to be borne, even in idea. The language of passion and exaggeration may silence that of sober reason in other places, it has not done it here. The question here is, whether the treaty be really so very fatal as to oblige the nation to break its faith...

It is in vain to allege that our faith plighted to France is violated by this new treaty. Our prior treaties are expressly saved from the operation of the British treaty. And what do those mean, who say that our honor was forfeited by treating at all, and especially by such a treaty? Justice, the laws and practice of nations, a just regard for peace as a duty to mankind, and the known wish of our citizens, as well as that self-respect which required it of the nation to act with dignity and moderation, all these forbade an appeal to arms before we had tried the effect of negotiation. The honor of the United States was saved, not forfeited by treating. The treaty itself by its stipulations for the posts, for indemnity, and for a due observation of our neutral rights, has justly raised the character of the nation. Never did the name of America appear in Europe with more lustre than upon the event of ratifying this instrument. The fact is of a nature to overcome all contradiction.

But the independence of the country—we are colonists again. This is the cry of the very men who tell us that France will resent our exercise of the rights of an independent nation to adjust our wrongs with an aggressor, without giving her the opportunity to say those wrongs shall subsist and shall not be adjusted. This is an admirable specimen of independence. The treaty with Great Britain, it cannot be denied, is unfavorable to this strange sort of independence....

Why do they complain that the West Indies are not laid open? Why do they lament that any restriction is stipulated on the commerce of the East Indies? Why do they pretend that if they reject this, and insist upon more, more will be accomplished? Let us be explicit—more would not satisfy. If all was granted, would not a treaty of amity with Britain still be obnoxious? Have we not this instant heard it urged against our envoy, that he was not ardent enough in his hatred of Great Britain? A treaty of amity is condemned because it was not made by a foe, and in the spirit of one. The same gentleman, at the same instant, repeats a very prevailing objection, that no treaty should be made with the enemy of France. No treaty, exclaim others, should be made with a monarch or a despot. There will be no naval security while those sea robbers domineer on the ocean. Their den must be destroyed. That nation must be extirpated.

THE BARBARY PIRATES

Americans today can hardly realize how weak the United States was in the 1790's when we had no navy whatsoever. The difficulties

The Age of Washington 1783-1801

of carrying out foreign policy under this circumstance may be seen in our dealings with the Barbary pirates. Soon after the Revolutionary War ended, the pirates began capturing American ships and holding the seamen for ransom. Without a navy, the United States had to pay.

In Washington's administration Congress appropriated nearly a million dollars to buy a peace treaty with the Barbary States, chief of which was Algiers. David Humphreys, American minister to Portugal, was charged with the negotiations, and he picked an old friend from Connecticut, Joel Barlow, who happened to be in business in France, to go to Algiers. The Dey of Algiers, who held more than 100 Americans as slaves, was willing to sell the United States a treaty, but when Barlow reached Africa, he encountered one problem after another.

As a young notion, besides having no navy, the United States also did not have much credit, and the task of raising money in Europe to pay for the treaty proved very difficult. The Dey, a temperamental dictator, insisted that the money be paid in gold. Barlow found that his problem in Algiers was not in negotiating the treaty but in keeping the Dey from declaring war on the United States before the money could be raised. In the letters that follow, Barlow reports to Humphreys and to the Secretary of State, Timothy Pickering, on his troubles. For a full account of this amazing episode in American history, see James Woodress, *A Yankee's Odyssey: The Life of Joel Barlow*, from which these letters are drown.

He first tells Pickering what happened when he reached Algiers in March, 1796:

I SENT him word that I was now consul and asked whether he would receive the customary consular present. This he refused and returned a menacing and insulting answer; and as the messenger was stooping to kiss his hand he struck him in the face.

The messenger at the same time delivered him a letter from Mr. Humphreys in answer to one he had written to Lisbon. He took it in his hand and threw it out the door with great fury uttering many execrations and threats. It was picked up and brought back to us, where it still remains unopened.

———◆———

> The Dey's wrath then subsided, and he apparently forgot about the Americans until early in April:

JOEL BARLOW TO DAVID HUMPHREYS IN LISBON:
                                                            Algiers, 3 April 1796
Sir:

THE Dey has this moment given us to understand that he has come to the following decision relative to our affair: that in eight days we shall be sent away from this place: that he will then allow thirty days but no more before his cruisers shall have orders to bring in American ships: that if in that time the money should arrive to pay the sums stipulated by Mr. Donaldson [Barlow's assistant, who had preceded him to Algiers], he will receive it and conclude the peace: otherwise it is war.

JOEL BARLOW TO DAVID HUMPHREYS:
                                                               Algiers, 5 April 1796
FOR two days past we have been witnesses to a scene of as complete and poignant distress as can be imagined, arising from the state of total despair in which our captives found themselves involved, and we without the power of administering the least comfort or hope. The threat which we mentioned in our last [letter] of sending us away had been reiterated with every mark of a fixed and final decision. And the Dey went so far as to declare that after the thirty days, if the money did not come, he never would be at peace with the Americans.

But the Dey did not carry out his threat just yet. Barlow thought of offering him as a gift a brand-new American war frigate. The skill of American shipbuilders was world famous, and the Dey was charmed by the prospect, like a child promised a new toy. He agreed to wait four months for his money. By the end of May, however, when the money had not yet arrived, the Dey began to get impatient again, and, worst of all, the plague broke out in Algiers. One American seaman fell ill and died, then another, and another. Barlow had to do something drastic, and his activities during the second week of July are recounted in the next two letters, both written the same day.

JOEL BARLOW TO THE SECRETARY OF STATE:

Algiers, 12 July 1796

Sir:

I HAVE the pleasure at last to announce to you the liberation of our people from slavery in this place. To keep the peace after the expiration time limited for the payment and finally to redeem our citizens, without any money, have been a subject of more difficulty and vexation than will be imagined by those who are unacquainted with the extremely capricious and savage character of the Dey.

A few weeks after the arrangement made in April, having heard nothing from the funds, and foreseeing that they probably would not be here by the time, I thought it highly expedient to engage the Dey in a step of his own by which he should be insensibly brought to consider the peace as established on a footing different from that of the punctuality of a moment in the payment of money.

> Barlow's letter goes on to explain in detail the stratagem he used to carry out this plan. It was sheer bluff, nerve, and shrewdness that saved the American prisoners. Barlow persuaded the influential Jewish banker Baccri to suggest to the Dey that he send

someone to Philadelphia to see about the annual tribute he was promised in the treaty. The Dey liked the idea and sent one of the American prisoners who had been acting as his secretary. Because Baccri was jealous of this prisoner, he was delighted to get rid of him and was obliged to Barlow for doing him a favor. Barlow thus gained time, because the Dey would now have to wait several months until his secretary could make a round trip to Philadelphia.

Soon after this event occurred, Barlow took advantage of the banker's pleasure in getting rid of the secretary and borrowed $200,000 from him to ransom the Americans. The banker did not have this much money himself but was able to borrow it from the Dey's own treasury. Hence the American seamen actually were ransomed by money which came out of the Dey's own pocket.

JOEL BARLOW TO THE SECRETARY OF STATE:

Algiers, 12 July 1796

Sir:

THIS will be presented to you by the remnant of our captive citizens who have survived the pains and humiliation of slavery in this place. After effecting their deliverance in the manner which I stated to you in my letter of this day, without funds or even any direct intelligence that they are soon to be expected, I have another task to perform in which it is impossible to promise myself success; it is to embark them without the infection of the plague.

Five of their fellow sufferers have died with that contagion within a few weeks, and another who is attacked must be left behind. It raged with such violence in the town, that although they cannot embark without risk, yet it is much more dangerous for them to stay longer here in any situation where it is possible for me to place them in this most incommodious of all conceivable abodes....

When we reflect on the extravagant sums of money that this redemption will cost the United States, it affords at least some consolation to know that it is not expended on worthless and disorderly persons, as is the case with some other nations who are driven, like us, to this humiliation to the Barbary States. Our people have conducted themselves in general with a degree of patience and decorum which would become a better condition than that of slaves.

Several of them are probably rendered incapable of gaining their living. One is in a state of total blindness; another is reduced nearly to the same condition; two or three carry the marks of unmerciful treatment in ruptures produced by hard labor; and others have had their constitutions injured by the plague.

> Not until the Americans were safely out of Algiers did the Dey discover the trick Barlow had played on him. He was furious and threatened dire punishments, but again Barlow's good luck, skillful diplomacy, and the friendship of Baccri, the banker, saved him. The American money to pay for the treaty, of course, arrived eventually, and Barlow then concluded treaties with the other Barbary states, Tripoli and Tunis, and returned to Paris.

V. The Adams Administration

WASHINGTON'S FAREWELL ADDRESS

The Jay Treaty of 1795 accentuated the differences between the Federalists and the Anti-Federalists. Those who supported the treaty were regarded as pro-British; those who opposed it were considered pro-French. By the time John Adams was elected President, the foreign policy debate had left deep scars. As early as 1792, Hamilton, in the same letter (quoted on page 41) that describes Jefferson, had said this about the Anti-Federalists: "They have a womanish attachment to France ad a womanish resentment against Great Britain. They would draw up into the closest embrace of the former, and involve us in all the consequences of her politics." On the other hand, the Jeffersonians believed that the Federalists hated France because the French Revolution had overthrown the king.

In 1797, George Washington retired to Mount Vernon and John Adams succeeded him as the second President. The tempo of war between France and the rest of Europe increased, and the battles of party politics at home became more and more partisan.

Washington's address was· written on the eve of Adams· election, just a few months before the new administration took office. John Adams was a man of competence and principle, but probably no President could have piloted the ship of state through the storms of the late eighteenth century without losing a few spars and sails. The advice to his countrymen that President Washington offered in the following selection was easier to give than to follow.

THE great rule of conduct for us, in regard to foreign nations is, in extending our commercial relations, to have with them as little political connection as possible. So far as we have already formed engagements, let them be fulfilled with perfect good faith. Here let us stop.

Europe has a set of primary interests, which to us have none, or a very remote relation. Hence she must be engaged in frequent controversies, the causes of which are essentially foreign to our concerns. Hence, therefore, it must be unwise in us to implicate ourselves, by artificial ties, in the ordinary vicissitudes of her politics, or the ordinary combinations and collisions of her friendships or enmities.

Our detached and distant situation invites and enables us to pursue a different course. If we remain one people, under an efficient government, the period is not far off when we may defy material injury from external annoyance; when we may take such an attitude as will cause the neutrality we may at any time resolve upon, to be scrupulously respected; when belligerent nations, under the impossibility of making acquisitions upon us, will not lightly hazard the giving us provocation; when we may choose peace or war, as our interest, guided by our justice, shall counsel.

Why forego the advantages of so peculiar a situation? Why quit our own, to stand upon foreign ground? Why, by interweaving our destiny with that of any part of Europe, entangle our peace and prosperity in the toils of European ambition, rivalship, interest, humor, or caprice?

'Tis our true policy to steer clear of permanent alliances with any portion of the foreign world, so far, I mean, as we are now at liberty to do it; for let me not be understood as capable of patronizing infidelity to existing engagements. I hold the maxim no less applicable to public than to private affairs that honesty is always the best policy.

I repeat, therefore, let those engagements be observed in their genuine sense. But, in my opinion, it is unnecessary, and would be unwise, to extend them.

Taking care always to keep ourselves, by suitable establishments, in a respectable defensive posture, we may safely trust to temporary alliances for extraordinary emergencies.

THE XYZ AFFAIR

The episode in American history known as the XYZ Affair erupted on the political horizon during the first year that President Adams was in office. Because the French revolutionary government resented the Jay Treaty between America and England, diplomatic relations between the United States and France deteriorated in 1797 almost to the point of war. Adams tried to restore harmonious relations by sending to France three emissaries, John Marshall, Charles C. Pinckney, and Elbridge Gerry to negotiate with the French government.

During their mission an astonishing proposition was made to them by three agents of the French government. Known only as X, Y, and Z, these agents proposed that the United States give a bribe to M. Talleyrand, the French Foreign Minister, and lend France a large sum of money. In return for this, France would be willing to conclude a new treaty of friendship to replace the old treaty which had been negotiated during the Revolutionary War. When this proposal was made public in the United States, it was rejected indignantly. Public opinion burned fiercely against France, and President Adams asked Congress to prepare for possible war.

The following selections illuminate various aspects of this remarkable affair. First is the report of the American emissaries describing their dealings with the mysterious Messieurs X, Y, and Z. This report was addressed to Timothy Pickering, Secretary of State.

In the morning of October the 18th, Mr. W. of the house of —— called on General Pinckney and informed him that a M. X., who was in Paris and whom the general had seen, was a gentleman of considerable credit and reputation...and that we might place great reliance on him.

In the evening of the same day, M. X. called on General Pinckney, and...whispered him that he had a message from M. Talleyrand to communicate when he was at leisure. General Pinckney immediately withdrew with him into another room, and when they were alone, M. X. said that he was charged with a business in which he was a novice, that he had been acquainted with M. Talleyrand, and that he was sure he had a great regard for [America] and its citizens and was very desirous that a reconciliation should be brought about with France; that, to effect that end, he was ready, if it was thought proper, to suggest a plan, confidentially, that M. Talleyrand expected would answer the purpose. General Pinckney said he should be glad to hear it. M. X. replied that the Directory [the committee of five men who governed France at this time], and particularly two of the members of it, were exceedingly irritated at some passages of the President's speech [to Congress attacking France], and desired that they should be softened; and that this step would be necessary previous to our reception. That, besides this, a sum of money was required for the pocket of the Directory and ministers which would be at the disposal of M. Talleyrand; and that a loan would also be insisted on. M.X. said if we acceded to these measures, M. Talleyrand had no doubt that all our differences with France might be accommodated. On inquiry, M. X. could not point out the particular passages of the speech that had given offence, nor the quantum of the loan, but mentioned that the *douceur* [*bribe*] for the pocket was twelve hundred thousand livres, about fifty thousand pounds sterling.

———•———

The General complained that to date he and his colleagues had been snubbed but that they wanted peace. He said he would consult with his colleagues about the proposition, which he wanted in writing. M. X. said he was not dealing directly with M. Talleyrand but with a friend of the foreign minister. It later developed that M. Talleyrand's friend was M. Y.

ON the morning of the 20th, M. X. called, and said that M. Y., the confidential friend of M. Talleyrand, instead of communicating with us through M. X. would see us himself and make the necessary explanations. We appointed to meet him on the evening of the 20th at seven o'clock in General Marshall's room. At seven, M. Y. and M. X. entered; and the first mentioned gentleman, being introduced to us as the confidential friend of M. Talleyrand, immediately stated to us the favorable impressions of that gentleman towards our country-impressions which were made by the kindness and civilities he had personally received in America. Impressed by his solicitude to repay these kindnesses, he was willing to aid us in the present negotiation by his good offices with the Directory, who were, he said, extremely irritated against the Government of the United States, on account of some parts of the President's speech, and who had neither acknowledged nor received us, and consequently have not authorized M. Talleyrand to have any communications with us. The minister therefore could not see us himself, but had authorized his friend M. Y. to communicate to us certain propositions, and to receive our answers to them, and to promise on his part, that if we would engage to consider them as the basis of the proposed negotiation, he would intercede with the Directory to acknowledge us and to give us a public audience. M. Y. stated to us, explicitly and repeatedly, that he was clothed with no authority; that he was not a diplomatic character; that he was only the friend of M. Talleyrand, and trusted by him.

Next we reprint Pickering's indignant comment on the affair in a letter he wrote to John Jay:

Philadelphia, April 9, 1798 Dear Sir:

Dir Sir:

THE dispatches from our envoys in Paris being published this morning, I do myself the pleasure to inclose you a copy. Unless the corruption of the French Government and their unjust, tyrannical, rapacious and insulting conduct towards the United States shall rouse the indignant spirit of the *people*, our independence is at an end. The leaders of the opposition in Congress, while thunderstruck with the exhibition of these dispatches, acknowledge the justice and moderation and sincerity of the Executive in his endeavours to accommodate our differences with France: but to all appearance, they will still oppose efficient measures even of defence, certainly by sea, and perhaps by land. Gallatin professes to believe that our envoys have entered on a negotiation, and that a treaty has ere this time been conducted. Mr. Jefferson says there is no evidence that the Directory had any knowledge of Talleyrand's unofficial negotiations!

Our final document on this affair is a letter Jefferson wrote to his nephew, Peter Carr, three days later. The publication of the proposal made by the French agents embarrassed Jefferson's party, which favored friendly relations with France. As you will see, Jefferson views the episode in quite a different light from Pickering and the Federalist administration.

As the instructions to our envoys and their communications have excited a great deal of curiosity, I enclose you a copy. You will perceive that they have been assailed by swindlers, whether with or without the participation of Talleyrand is not very apparent. The known corruption of his character renders it very possible he may have intended to share largely in the fifty thousand pounds demanded. But that the Directory knew anything of it is neither proved nor probable. On the contrary, when the Portuguese ambassador yielded to like attempts of swindlers, the conduct of the Directory in imprisoning him for an attempt at corruption, as well as their general conduct, really magnanimous, places them above suspicion.

It is pretty evident that Mr. A's speech is in truth the only obstacle to negotiation, that humiliating disavowals of that are demanded as a preliminary, or as a commutation for that, a heavy sum of money, about a million sterling. This obstacle removed, they seem not to object to an arrangement of all differences, and even to settle and acknowledge themselves debtors for spoliations [confiscating American ships]. Nor does it seem that negotiation is at an end, as the President's message says, but that it is in its commencement only.

John Adams had much trouble restraining his party's hotheads who wanted to go to war with France, and at the cost of his political future he sent another emissary to France to resume the broken-off negotiations. His enemies within the Federalist Party, led by Alexander Hamilton, were furious with him, and the fight inside the party over this issue wrecked it. Adams' second try at negotiation with France succeeded, and war was averted. Before the trouble ended, however, Congress created a navy, the United States fought a small undeclared war at sea with France, and George Washington was called out of retirement to lead the army again, if need be.

THE ALIEN AND SEDITION ACTS

In 1798, when war with France appeared likely, the Adams administration tried to hush the noisy Republican opposition by pushing through Congress the notorious Alien and Sedition Acts. One of these laws forbade any person to "write, print, utter, or publish...any false, scandalous, and malicious writing or writings against the government of the United States." This act could have meant the end of free speech as guaranteed by the Bill of Rights. Under the provisions of this law any Republican who publicly opposed the government's policies could be jailed.

Scores of Jefferson's followers were arrested, and some were sent to prison in the months that followed the passage of these laws. Adams' critics were hard to silence, however, particularly Congressman Matthew Lyon of Vermont, who loved a political battle. He deliberately published a private letter Joel Barlow had written his brother-in-law, Senator Baldwin. Among other things, Barlow had said that Adams was acting like a madman in his conduct of diplomatic relations with France. In publishing this letter Lyon was daring the Federalists to prosecute him. They did.

In the selection that follows, Lyon writes Senator Mason of Virginia from jail describing his trial and imprisonment. We have used only part of what is a very long letter.

As to the second count several evidences were brought to swear they heard me read the letter, said to be the letter from a diplomatic character in France, from a manuscript copy, supposed to be in my own handwriting; they were inquired of whether the reading of the letter caused any tumult. One of the evidences, a young lawyer, and another person, an associate of his, said that they thought it did at Middletown. One of them said he heard a person say, there must be a revolution, and they both agreed that there was a noise—and some tumult after the reading of that letter and some other papers. On my inquiring of them the cause of the tumult, and their opinion, if there would have been any tumult there, if they had not followed me on purpose to make a disturbance? they acknowledged, they thought if they had not been there, there would have been no disturbance; and they also agreed, that the tumult was caused by the other people's disliking their being there, and their conduct then; they agreed also that I refused to give an opinion upon the letter.

The attorney proceeded to sum up the evidence, and dwelt on everything which he thought proper to point out the appearance of evil intentions. As soon as he had seated himself, or before Judge Paterson rose and was proceeding to give his charge to the jury, I interrupted him with an inquiry into the cause why I should not be heard; he politely sat down and directed me to proceed. My defense consisted of an appeal to the jury on the unconstitutionality of the law, the innocence of the passage in my letter, and the innocence of the manner in which I read the letter. It was said I spoke two hours and upwards....The jury retired about eight o'clock in the evening, and in about an hour they returned with a verdict, *Guilty!* The Judge... pronounced sentence that I be imprisoned four calendar months, pay a fine of one thousand dollars, and stand committed until the judgment should be complied with. This sentence was unexpected to all my friends as well as myself; no one expected imprisonment...

After the court adjourned, I inquired what was to be done with me until my commitment. I expected I should he confined in the prison in Rutland, the county where I lived; I was told that the marshal was authorized to imprison me in what jail in the State he pleased, and that I must go to Vergennes, about forty-four miles north of Rutland, and about the same distance from my scat al Fair Haven. I inquired what were the accommodations there? and was answered in a manner peculiar to the marshal himself, that they were very good. I told the marshal, since it had become my duty to go there, he needed no assistance, I would go with him. He said he would not trust to that, and prepared two troopers, with their pistols to guard me. He ordered me to ride just before them; in this manner I left Rutland.

After riding a few miles he overtook us and rode by us; he rode pretty fast and whispered to one of the young men; I learned his intention was, to get to Middlebury, the shire town of Addison county, in order to throw me into a dirty dungeon-like room for that night. I did not mend my pace; he came back and scolded; insulted and threatened; he repeated it. His friends, I was told, expostulated with him, and the humane young men, who were employed as guards, told him they would rather watch me all night than that I should be thrown into the jail; we lived at a tavern about four miles short of Middlebury jail; the young men watched.

The next day we arrived at this place; there are two roads to come into it, one comes up straight to the jail-house, by but two or three houses; the other is circuitous, taking almost the whole length of the little city in its course. I was foremost and inclined to take the nearest road, but the *gentleman*, by that route, would lose a share of his triumph; he ordered us in a peremptory tone into the circuitous road through the city. On the way from Rutland, he undertook to direct me, and stop me as to speaking, and told me I should not have the use of pen, ink and paper.

On Wednesday evening last I was locked up in this room, where I now am; it is about sixteen feet long by twelve wide, with a necessary [toilet] in one corner, which affords a stench about equal to the Philadelphia docks in the month of August. This cell is the common receptacle for horse-thieves, money-makers, runaway Negroes, or any kind of felons. There is a half-moon hole through the door, sufficient to receive a plate through, and for my friends to look through and speak to me. There is a window place on the opposite side, about twenty inches by sixteen, crossed by nine square iron bars; all the light I have is through this aperture; no fire-place in the cell, nor is there anything but the iron bars to keep the cold out; consequently I have to walk smartly with my great coat on, to keep comfortably warm some mornings....

On Friday, for the first time, two brothers-in-law were admitted to come in to see me. Some of my friends expostulated with the marshal on the subject of denying me pen and ink; and in the evening I observed a man hammering on the prison door. You seem much concerned about that door (said I); there has scarce been an hour since I came here, but there has been some person hammering at the door, or putting on new bolts or bars. It is all useless, said I; if I wished to come out, they could not hold me; and as I do not, if my limits were marked by a single thread, I would not overstep it. He replied, he was only nailing up an advertisement.

The Federalists had a lion by the tail in the Alien and Sedition Acts. The public sided with the Vermont Congressman and other Jeffersonians prosecuted under these laws, and the harshness of this legislation certainly proved a major factor in the election of Jefferson as President in 1800. So indignant were the Vermont voters at the political nature of Matthew Lyon's prosecution that they re-elected him to Congress by a large majority even while he was in jail serving his sentence.

About the Editors

RICHARD BRANDON MORRIS (1904-1989) was an American historian best known for his pioneering work in colonial American legal history and the early history of American labor. In 1924, received a BA degree from City College and completed an MA from Columbia Law School the following year. He earned a PhD in history at Columbia University where he eventually became the Gouverneur Morris Professor of History. In later years, he shifted his research interests to the constitutional, diplomatic, and political history of the American Revolution and the making of the United States Constitution. In 1966 Morris won the Bancroft Prize in History for his book on the diplomacy of the American Revolution, *The Peacemakers: The Great Powers and American Independence* (1965). He edited the papers of John Jay and published a biography, *John Jay, the Nation, and the Court*, focusing on Jay's work as a diplomat and as the first Chief Justice of the United States. Morris's 1966 book *The American Revolution Reconsidered* was followed in 1970 by his *The Emerging Nations and the American Revolution*. In 1973, preparing for the impending bicentennial of the American Revolution, he published a collection of biographical essays in *Seven Who Shaped Our Destiny: The Founding Fathers as Revolutionaries*.

JAMES LESLIE WOODRESS (1916-2011) was a literary biographer and historian in the field of American literature. After earning his bachelor's degree at Amherst College and his master's at New York University, he served in the U.S. Army during World War II. He completed his doctoral dissertation at Duke University, which led to the publication of his first book *Howells and Italy*. In the 1950s until the mid 1960s, he taught in the English Department at California State University, Northridge (originally San Fernando Valley State College). There he served as department chair and as Dean of the School of Humanities. He continued his career at the University of California, Davis, until his retirement in 1987. Woodress wrote two biographies of Willa Cather, *Willa Cather: Her Life and Art* and *Willa Cather: A Literary Life*. The second of these books, described in the New York Times as "the most cogent, balanced biography of Cather to date," contributed significantly to the high reputation that Cather currently holds among American authors. He also wrote biographies of Joel Barlow and Booth Tarkington. He was the founder of *American Literary Scholarship*, a distinguished annual review of literary criticism. In 1985 the Modern Language Association awarded him its Hubbell Medal for his significant contributions to the study and teaching of American literature.

FIRSTHAND HISTORY

Jamestown to Washington's Farewell 1607-1801
Jefferson's America to The Civil War 1801-1865
Rebuilding the Union to The First World War 1865-1920
The Roaring Twenties to the Cold War 1920-1961

www.ingramcontent.com/pod-product-compliance
Lightning Source LLC
Chambersburg PA
CBHW031639040426
42453CB00006B/156